HINTERLAND

Hinterland offers an ans[wer] [to the]
question 'what is creativ[e non-fiction]'
by showcasing the best n[ew writing in]
the fields of memoir, essay, travel and
food writing, reportage, psychoscape,
biography, flash non-fiction and more.

Our pages bring together work by
established, award-winning authors
alongside new writers, many of whom
we are thrilled to publish for the first time
and whose work, we promise, will merit
your full attention.

Often, the pieces you'll find in Hinterland
will straddle the boundaries between
strands and be difficult to classify:
we see this as a strength. Hinterland
intends to challenge, move, entertain
and, above all, be a fantastic read.

WELCOME TO ISSUE 1

Advocates for Hinterland:
Trevor Goul-Wheeker, Nathan Hamilton, Rachel Hore,
Kathryn Hughes, Helen Smith, Rebecca Stott, Ian Thomson

Editorial Team
Editors-In-Chief – Freya Dean & Andrew Kenrick
Art Direction & Design – Tom Hutchings
Business Support – Ben Watkins
Readers – Susan K Burton, Aaron Deary, Margaret Hedderman,
Yin F Lim, Aaron O'Farrell, Stephen Massil

Submissions
Hinterland is committed to paying writers and artists for all work we publish.
Please send us your work via Submittable:
hinterlandnonfiction.submittable.com
We accept submissions year-round and endeavour to reply within 3 months.
We regret we are unable to provide feedback.
There is a small fee of £3 per submission.

Subscriptions
An annual subscription to Hinterland
(four issues, print and digital) costs £34 U.K.,
£44 Europe, £54 Rest-of-world.
Digital subscription only, £20.
Please visit our website for full details.

Distribution
Hinterland is distributed worldwide by NBN International.
For all trade orders contact +44 (0) 1752 202301
orders@nbninternational.com

Advertising
Please see our website for current rates, or to discuss sponsorship please
contact Andrew Kenrick at hinterlandnonfiction@gmail.com

Acknowledgments
The Editors gratefully acknowledge financial contributions from the UEA
Enterprise Santander fund and support from the UEA Publishing Project.

Find Hinterland online at
www.hinterlandnonfiction.com
or contact us: hinterlandnonfiction@gmail.com

ISBN: 978-1-911343-85-1
ISSN (Print): 2632-136X
ISSN (Online): 2632-1378

HINTERLAND

THE BEST NEW CREATIVE NON-FICTION

Issue 1
SPRING
2019

Issue 1 / Spring 2019

Editorial

Welcome to this first issue of Hinterland, a magazine dedicated to the best new creative non-fiction.

The world of non-fiction publishing has grown enormously in recent years – works of memoir, reportage, science, history, biography, food, landscape and travel writing, all have come to dominate our shelves. Many of the most popular among these straddle genres, carving out a remarkable hinterland within the world of writing.

However where to find such writing before it arrives in the form of a bestseller? Our hope is that each issue of Hinterland will provide exactly this: a platform from which we can champion the best non-fiction writers from around the world, allowing new and upcoming authors the opportunity to have their work published – some of them for the very first time – alongside award-winning names; and to give you, our readers, a ready place to discover that talent.

So where do we find our authors? As a new publisher, we'd like to be transparent about the way we source our content. We are both alumni of the University of East

Freya Dean is of Dutch-British descent. She was an Elizabeth Kostova Foundation Finalist in 2017 and the recipient of the 2017/2018 Lorna Sage Award. Her work has appeared in *Visual Verse*, *The Writes of Woman* and *UEA's NonFiction Anthology*.

Anglia's famed creative writing programme, so we are not short of talented peers – this issue features new work by five recent graduates of UEA, along with two award-winning members of the faculty. However the remaining nine authors featured in these pages were entirely unknown to us when we began work on Hinterland – theirs is writing that we received via our open call on Submittable. Of those nine contributors, four are making their print debut with us – we're confident it won't be their last. Another detail of which we are proud: every one of our contributors is being paid for their work.

We share this information because for some the publishing industry remains opaque and the route to publication obscure. We hope that, in outlining the way we work, writers of all experience might be encouraged to submit to Hinterland, knowing that we will be eager to read their work; and for you to feel confident that the writing we publish really is among the very best in new creative non-fiction.

Freya Dean & Andrew Kenrick
Editors-in-Chief

Andrew Kenrick has worked as an archaeologist and an archivist, a writer and an editor. He is currently studying for a PhD at the University of East Anglia, where he is researching new ways to write biographies of ancient figures.

Contributors

Susan Karen Burton
(*A Hostess of the Floating World*)
lived and worked in Japan for
14 years before completing
doctorates in history and in
creative-critical writing. Her
work has appeared in *Times
Higher Education, The Telegraph,
The Manchester Review, Words
and Women* and *Going Down
Swinging.* She is the co-author
of two books in Japanese and,
in 2018, a work in progress,
*Gaijin: Modern Japan Through
Western Eyes*, was shortlisted
for the Tony Lothian Prize.

Amy Cotler (*Hazeri*)
worked as a chef, cookery
teacher, food writer and
advocate in New York and
New England, where she
was the founding director of
Berkshire Grown, an early
farm-to-table initiative that
received national recognition.
She has authored five
culinary books and hosted
a web column for *The New
York Times*. Forthcoming
is a novel-length memoir,
*Unexpected Pleasures, Tales from
a Culinary Alchemist.* Amy
currently lives in Mexico.
Visit her at amycotler.com

Scott Coykendall
(*Sabbatical Report*) is a professor at Plymouth State University in New Hampshire, where he teaches Journalism, Technical Communication, and other writing courses. His poems have appeared in *COG*, *Black Fox Literary Magazine*, *The Cossack Review*, and *The 2River View*, among others. This is his first published non-fiction piece.

Randal Doane
(*Confidence Game*) works as a copywriter in Northeast Ohio. Randal is the author of the award-winning *Stealing All Transmissions: A Secret History of The Clash*, which is a love story about four lads and a city named New York, as well as a segment of rock'n'roll history. He's written on music and culture for *Alternative Press*, *Louder Than War* and *Harper's*. Chilled martini glasses remain his favorite social media platform.

Eileen Favorite
(*O, Garbage Men! and Holy Well*)
Eileen's first novel, *The Heroines*, was translated into six languages. Her essays, poems and stories have appeared in many publications, including *The Toast*, *Triquarterly*, *The Rumpus* and *Diagram*. She has received fellowships from the Illinois Arts Council for poetry and for prose and currently teaches writing and literature classes at the School of the Art Institute of Chicago.

Peter Goulding (*Hogiau Pen Garret*) is a climber and writer from the North of England. He has spent most of his working life in kitchens, pubs and on building sites. He now lives in rural Norfolk. He is working on *Slatehead*, a history and memoir of the North Wales climbing scene.

Tom Hutchings is our in-house graphic designer and photographer, based in the south of London. When not wrangling words into columns or distressing letterforms, he's often found board gaming or painting miniatures. Have a look at his varied output at www.thorngraphicdesign.com

Helen James (*Cullerfornia*) began her career as a photographer in the North West of England before working as an educator at the National Portrait Gallery, Open Eye Gallery and Photoworks. She currently works as an associate lecturer at the University of Westminster, where she teaches 'writing photography.' Helen's own writing focuses on the interplay of words and images; and often responds to the landscapes that have featured as backdrops in her life. Her son Calumn James is a surfer and maker of wooden things based in North Shields.

Joshua Jones (*Dreamscape*) is an illustrator based in Cambridge, who specialises in traditional media and dabbles in digital illustration. Alongside his editorial artwork, Josh has collaborated on a wide range of projects, including band posters, indie board games and scientific infographics. If he's not drawing Josh is probably playing D&D, or walking his dog. Find him online at www.joshuajonesprojects.com

Justin Kern (*Second Time Around*) is a former daily news reporter who currently lives in Milwaukee. His words have appeared in *Utne Reader*, *Great Lakes Review*, *Forth*, *Wanderlust Journal*, *Longshot Island*, *Milwaukee Record* and a trio of anthologies from *Belt Publishing*. Justin is also a lifelong amateur musician who throws horseshoes as a phony spiritual exercise.

Michael Kineman (*American Boys Are Fast But Not As Fast As Ginger Boys*) is an Anglo-American, born in the Midwestern United States but raised and educated in the British West Midlands. During his twenties, Michael worked in human rights law and taught English in the Far East before studying creative writing at the University of East Anglia. Memory, third-culture identity and religious doubt are common themes in his writing. He is currently at work on his first book, *The Fields We Used to Roam*.

Damian Le Bas
(*In Conversation With*)
is a writer and occasional
filmmaker from West Sussex.
His first book, *The Stopping
Places: a Journey through Gypsy
Britain*, is an exploration
of Gypsy and Traveller
history told through a year
spent travelling around
the country's old nomadic
halting sites. It won a Royal
Society of Literature Jerwood
Award for Non-fiction, was
a BBC Radio 4 'Book of the
Week', and was shortlisted for
the Stanford Dolman Travel
Book of the Year.

Scott Russell Morris
(*Just Like Home*) is a faculty
member at the University of
Utah Asia Campus. His work
has appeared in *Brevity*, *The
Chattahoochee Review*, *Superstition
Review* and elsewhere.

Saloni Prasad (*The Women
At The Station*) is from Surat,
India. She writes about life,
people and culture; likes to
listen to Indian Classical
music and can often be
spotted talking to herself.
She recently completed her
Masters in creative writing
at the University of East
Anglia in Norwich. In her
former life, she was a project
manager and an electrical
engineer. Saloni blogs at
www.theturquoiseink.com

Josef Steiff (*Flashpoint*)
is a former licensed social
worker from Appalachia. Josef
creates films, installations,
performance and written
work that reflect his interest
in the ways that people
struggle to make sense of
impersonal events. His films
have been exhibited in the
United States, Europe and
Asia; his creative non-fiction
has appeared in *Batayan*, the
forthcoming *Pikeville Review*
and via the independent
publishing house *Open Court*.

Rebecca Stott (*The Fall*) is a novelist, broadcaster and historian. She has written several books of creative non-fiction including *Darwin and the Barnacle*, *Darwin's Ghosts* and most recently a memoir, *In the Days of Rain*, which won the Costa Biography Prize 2017. Rebecca is Professor of Literature and Creative Writing at the University of East Anglia, and is currently writing a novel set in the ruins of sixth-century Londinium.

Ian Thomson (*Blue Murder*) is the author of an acclaimed biography of Primo Levi, a study of Dante and two prize-winning works of reportage, *Bonjour Blanc: A Journey Through Haiti* and *The Dead Yard: Tales of Modern Jamaica*. He also edited *Articles of Faith: The Collected Tablet Journalism of Graham Greene*. Ian is the recipient of the Royal Society of Literature's Ondaatje Prize and the W.H. Heinemann Award.

Daniel Uncapher (*Yocknapatafa*) is a Sparks Fellow at Notre Dame, where he received his MFA. His work has appeared or is forthcoming in *Chicago Quarterly Review*, *The Carolina Quarterly*, *Penn Review*, *Tin House Online*, and others.

Leo Vanderpot (*Brief Lives*) lives in Croton-on-Hudson, New York. In recent years, his poems, stories and essays have appeared in fewer journals than he anticipated. He therefore bows to the exceptionally engaging discernment of *Hinterland*. Praise or slate him: leovl0571@yahoo.com

HINTERLAND

At Hinterland we are committed to publishing the best in creative non-fiction from around the globe.

We are always thrilled to feature work from established, well-known authors but have a particular interest in discovering new voices and in pieces that sit outside the usual categories: we ask only that it be a work of non-fiction.

We operate an open, year-round submissions policy and aim to read all work submitted within three months.

We pay for all the work that we publish and receive frequent interest from agents and publishers regarding our contributors.

Please send us your best work and we will endeavour to find a place for it.

Guidelines for submissions

- Submissions should be made via Submittable only. Please follow the link below..

- A small fee of £3 per submission applies to non-subscribers. Subscribers enjoy the benefit of submitting their work for free.

- All work should be new, previously unpublished material. If your work is subsequently accepted elsewhere, please kindly let us know.

- Pieces should not run to more than 5000 words. We accept anything from 500 words (very short pieces will be considered for our flash non-fiction slot). We also accept extracts from longer works, or works in progress.

- We warmly embrace writing on any topic, or from any genre, we ask only that it falls somewhere in the realm of non-fiction writing.

- Your work will be considered for all upcoming issues; it might help you to know that we operate a 3-4 month editorial lead time.

- We regret that, due to the number of submissions received, we cannot provide feedback.

hinterland.submittable.com/submit

Announcing the inaugural

HINTERLAND
Prize 2019

Creative Non-fiction Contest

Awarding

£500 first prize
+ mentoring session with A.M. Heath Literary Agency

£200 second prize

£100 third prize

To be judged by

Kathryn Hughes	**Euan Thorneycroft**	**The Editors of Hinterland**
Award-winning Author, Journalist and Professor of Life Writing at the University of East Anglia	Literary Agent at A.M. Heath, London	and a peer review panel, to include recent graduates of UEA's famed Creative Writing MA program

Accepting non-fiction pieces of up to 5000 words (no minimum)
Submission period open 28th May – 2nd July 2019

Full prize details and how to enter, please see:
www.hinterlandnonfiction.com/prize

Barbara Kingsolver

Kingsolver

Letter
19.2 a9

February 11, 1999

> And yet, I feel that everything I write is constructed to carry a message. Maybe not a *moral* outright, like Aesop's fables, but a meaning within a moral context. Why write it, otherwise? God knows there are enough clever sentences already piled up in the libraries collecting dust.

Barbara Kingsolver

Letter from Barbara Kingsolver to Doris Lessing

In late 1998 the American author Barbara Kingsolver
visited the British writer Doris Lessing at her home
in London. They had tea and talked of cats, African
politics and Lessing expressed dissatisfaction with
her own short story 'Hunger,' overly laboured, as she
felt it to be, in attempting to deliver both narrative
and a moral. Shortly afterwards, Kingsolver wrote
to thank Lessing and picked up on the idea of story
as communication – offering an intimate glimpse
into her preoccupations as a writer.

Kingsolver had recently published *The Poisonwood
Bible*. Although a work of fiction it dealt absolutely
in real-world themes, at its core the damaging
legacy of colonialisation. It was the book that would
go on to secure Kingsolver's place as one of the
great contemporary American writers, garnering
multiple awards including, in April of that year,
Finalist in the Pulitzer Prize for Letters and the
following year, winner of the National Humanities
Medal. Alongside her fiction writing, Kingsolver
has produced numerous works of non-fiction,
including *Animal, Vegetable, Miracle: A Year of Food Life*,
which won the James Beard Award for Writing and
the Indies Choice Book Award for Adult Nonfiction.
She is a writer who steps effortlessly from one genre
to another and whose work, as her letter to Lessing
reveals, is concerned above all with message. **H**

Letter from the Doris Lessing Archive, at the British Archive for Contemporary Writing, UEA
© Barbara Kingsolver, reprinted by kind permission of The Frances Goldin Literary Agency.

Confidence Game

Randal Doane

It's eight ball at the pool table at the back of the bar.
Skinny boys slouch akimbo in flannel and denim
and Doc Martens. 'Nice shot,' one of them harps,
and drops the butt of a hand-rolled cigarette into an
abandoned pint glass. I sink the three ball, and the
seven ball, and roll the two ball along the side rail,
short at the corner pocket. 'So. Close,' he whispers.

I started playing pool at the age of seven, in the
summer of '76; eight ball almost always. My family
followed my father's work to Jackson, Michigan, and
his workdays often concluded with meetings at Mr
Miller's house. I tagged along to play pool. House
rules were few, but inflexible. Call your shots: no slop
allowed. Sink the cue ball or 'scratch'? Place one of
your sunk balls on the foot spot. Scratch on the eight
ball? You lose. Zach, the eldest of the Miller kids,
taught me how to apply backspin to the cue ball,
to avoid scratches on side-pocket shots, to calculate
angles and force, to think one and eventually two
shots ahead. I was skinny, even spindly, and lacked
the strength to transfer enough oomph from my
stick to the cue ball, to the 15-ball pyramid.

After my first victory, I honored the edict of
winner's break. I drove my stick across my guide hand,
its tip clipped the top of the cue ball, which scooted
slowly into a glancing kiss at the tip of the triangle.

The balls shivered, but hardly budged. The cue ball eased to a stop. 'Oh!,' Zach noted. 'We can start again, if you'd like, and I'll break.' I nodded, smiled, and quickly re-racked the balls. The Millers' table was pristine. It yielded honest, sometimes humbling, results. I enjoyed the sound of a ball well struck, the sight of spheres glossy and spinning. Joint exercises of geometry and physics, good angles and right energy emptied the table. Sloppy stick work did not.

I walk around to the other side of the table. 'Side pocket,' I note and nod. The cue ball greets the eight ball and scoots backwards. The eight ball rolls across the table and over the lip of the pocket.

'All right! Let's play!' barks the mouthy boy, and he jams his quarters into the slot. 'About time!' He gathers the balls and slides the triangle's nose up, back, and onto its mark. 'OK, OK!' he splutters. I position the cue ball and draw back my stick. Crack! The balls scatter, collide, roll and stop. 'Nice break,' he says, surprised. 'Which ball fell?'

I tally the solids, then the stripes. 'The eight ball,' I note, and direct my gaze away from the table and pause. The eight ball, off the break? I've never seen it. Never considered it. I face the chalkboard and its queue of names. I meet the mouthy boy's gaze and hold it. I smile. I bluff. 'Next,' I say, smiling, and watch another skinny boy pull a stack of quarters from his pocket. ◨

Hazeri

Amy Cotler

It's easy to imagine surfing from childhood into
the life of a young adult on a wave of pork. Our
household of secular Jewish immigrants ate it with
gusto. My maternal grandfather mumbling '*chaza*'
(*haaza*), a Yiddish word for forbidden pork, in a stage
whisper, with a strong guttural *haaa* before gobbling
it up. On the other side, my favorite great-aunt, Ida,
who kept kosher at home, savored pork at Chinese
restaurants only. Her secret? 'Don't look too closely.'

At home my mother never cooked boney pork
chops. Those I discovered at my friend's strangely
polite family dinner as 'that fabulous meat with a
bone.' Perhaps fragrant, fat-spattering, un-smoked
pork was deemed too porky. Or simply, it wasn't the
pork of my parents' childhood.

But still, we devoured bacon and ham.

Bacon appeared on little rolls for morning
breakfast, the fat 'n' salt mouthful doing a yin-yang
dance with its ever-so-sweet and spongy bun. Years
later, my grown-up baby sister spoke wistfully of
those breakfasts while preparing her daughter's hasty
jam and toast on her way to an endless work day.

In the green suburbs of our youth, there was
always time for pork. Food was abundant, but pork,
a meat forbidden in our recent past, was especially
tasty. My mother marinated Craig Claiborne's pork
satay with Brazil nuts, soy sauce and lemon, which

was always accompanied with skinny pake noodles tossed in butter and toasted sesame seeds.

I sat on my usual perch – a stool pushed against the kitchen island – waiting for the choice pieces, which were slightly charred on the outside, permeated with mysterious flavors from afar. How could the meat from one animal contain such varied flavors?

Household parties often called for ham, displayed whole on a giant wooden carving platter. Sliced off the bone onto plates by guests, always served with a small bowl of grainy mustard. And, of course, the bone was used later for thick split pea soup.

Years later, too early in the romance for such intimate gifts, I brought my new love a soup bone, remnant from one of my first catering jobs in the big city. I'd served the ham from which it came, thinly sliced on little cream biscuits with that same grainy mustard my mom favored. The ham was bought at the pork butcher on 9th Avenue, one of the many miracles of Manhattan, with the rump bone removed for easy slicing. It was one of four hams that my new helper, a young cousin, carved for that gig, a job that sent her right back to college. Not so for me. The standing, the repetitive slicing, accompanied by the salty smell, the occasional nibble and strains of Billie Holiday – my place, my choice of music – gave me immense pleasure.

My love had Irish roots, salt and pepper his mother's only seasoning ingredients. But they ate pork as often as they could afford it, and potatoes at almost every meal. And so, at first to please him, I was introduced once again to succulent pork roast on its bone, this time, where it belongs. Some evenings its aroma defined the Lower Manhattan loft where we eventually lived together, filling our kitchen before drifting down the stairs, stopped only by the heavy metal door at the entrance. ⬛

O, Garbage Men!

Eileen Favorite

We used to chase the garbage men down the street. The boys on the block liked to watch the jaws of the truck smashing the garbage. We girls tagged along after them. One day, I was standing next to a metal trashcan. I couldn't have been more than five years old. A garbage man grabbed me around the waist and said, 'Now, who would throw away this little dolly?' I was airborne in his gloved hands. He held me over the dirty hatch of the powder-blue garbage truck. He was about to throw me into the stinking mouth of it, into the rotten food, the meat bones, the cans and bottles that nobody knew they should recycle yet. The mangled wet newspapers. I yelled, 'I'm a real girl, mister! I'm a real girl!' ▐

Brief Lives

'*Sometimes the most important thing a critic leaves behind is a singular, wised-up, cant-free voice that is pure intelligence at play, and at its best Macdonald's voice shoots off the page as if he were broadcasting live and cutting through the static.*'
— James Walcott, On Dwight Macdonald,
New York Times, April 16, 2006

Two Journal Entries

by Leo Vanderpot

Saturday, February 18th, 2012
Nooshing around the www, I see my name attached
to the Yale University Library, to which a few
years ago I donated two letters I had received
from Dwight Macdonald. The goofiness of the
Provenance section is a joy for me, but I am not sure
how it can be accurate:

> 'Purchased from Dwight Macdonald, 1974-
> 1978; and Mrs. Macdonald, 1984-1985. Gift
> of Leonard Vanderpot, 2009.'

Can it be that only D.M., Mrs. Macdonald and
myself have submitted (or sold) material to this
collection? Best company I have ever been in!

I recall reading that Macdonald sold his papers to Yale for fifteen thousand dollars (a large sum in the 1970s), which he was proud of, since his life-long dictum 'Don't throw it out' had turned into income as well as a safe home at his alma mater. Macdonald is not so well known these days as he was when I first read his work in the 1950s. For the better part of four decades, from the mid 1930s well into the 1970s, he was a leading editor, essayist, critic (books and movies) and political analyst. Blake Bailey, in his biography of John Cheever, points out that in one year (1958) Macdonald as a critic caused a dramatic, if not fatal, decline in the reputation of America's best-selling novelist James Gould Cozzens (*By Love Possessed*) and launched the reputation of James Agee, whose posthumously published novel, *Let Us Now Praise Famous Men*, won the Pulitzer prize that same year.

In October 1967, Norman Mailer agreed to take part in what became known as The March on the Pentagon, a huge anti-Vietnam War rally in Washington, D.C. Mailer urged Macdonald and Robert Lowell to join him, which they did, allowing Mailer to say that in the front rank of the march he had, as our leading novelist, been accompanied by our leading poet and our leading critic.

Macdonald first wrote to me in answer to a letter I had sent him regarding a movie review – he had written something about *Citizen Kane* that I disagreed with. The second letter concerned something of historical interest. I had forwarded to Macdonald a clipping from the *New York Herald Tribune*, a story on how, after the assassination of JFK, Lyndon Johnson, as the incumbent President, worked with Kennedy staff members to continue several programs that had been in various stages of development. The Tribune reporter focused his piece on 'The War on Poverty' and pointed out that President Kennedy became eager to take action on the topic after one of his staff members gave him a copy of Macdonald's New Yorker review of Michael Harrington's book *The Other America: Poverty in the United States*, which appeared in the magazine's January 19 issue, 1963.

Macdonald wrote a note thanking me – he had no knowledge that anyone in the Kennedy administration had read his review, which must be one of the most politically influential pieces of criticism ever to appear in print, ranking in importance with those famous books that first emerged from the pages of The New Yorker: Janet Malcolm's *The Journalist and the Murderer*, Rachel Carson's *Silent Spring*, John Hersey's *Hiroshima*, and Hannah Arendt's *Eichmann in Jerusalem*.

Sunday, November 4, 2012
Over to Bard College at 2.30 for a concert – canceled because of Hurricane Sandy, also the reason the New York City Marathon was not run today. This is the night we turn back our clocks, so with the extra hour provided I pick through the 8-inch square cardboard box that is the last to be dealt with after my move to this apartment in June. The box contains hundreds of vocabulary cards that I made in college and beyond – quotations on the front of the cards, definitions on

the back. Three come easily to hand, all taken from the writings of Dwight Macdonald. (The first card is hand-written, the second and third typewritten.)

> (1) '400 Blows is best told chronologically because it is a story of the development of youth, a bildungsroman but in a reverse direction: devolution rather than evolution is the point.'

This was most likely from *Esquire* magazine, for which Macdonald wrote a monthly movie column. I remember he said of 400 Blows that it was not a great film, but it was a film that would perhaps prove to be one of the best films of that year. The www reveals that this Truffaut production was released in 1959. I was in the fourth of six years it took to earn my BS at Boston University.

> (2) (Writing on James Agee) 'Time Inc. is not really an abattoir because [we] took its paychecks [...] unlike the cattle, of our own free will.'

> (3) 'After a century and a half of romanticism, culminating in such solipsistic excesses as action painting and beat writing, it is easy to forget that a work of art is impersonal fabrication as well as personal expression.'

Brown and frayed envelopes are marked with the dates when I diligently revisited their contents, informal academic brush-ups from 1961 to 1970.

I revisit some of the cards contained therein:

(In the forecourt of Saint Mark's) '[...] like an open-air salon dedicated to cooling drink and to a still finer degustation - that of exquisite impressions received during the day.'

– Henry James, *The Aspern Papers*

From E.E. Cummings' book *I*: 'The more implacably a virtuous Cambridge drew me toward what might have been her bosom, the more sure I felt that soi-disant respectability comprised nearly everything which I couldn't respect, and the more eagerly I explored sinful Somerville.'

One card revealed the spirit of the whole box. On the front: 'thallus, plural thalli (Found roaming in Webster).' On the back: 'plants: like green slime, or mold that does not have distinguishable body, branches and roots. Some are one cell and asexual.'

Roaming in Webster. I put that on my list of things done and things to do.

There is a stack of cards which all refer to the works of John Milton, notes taken during a course taught by Edward Wagenknecht at Boston University. Larger cards, beyond the 3X5 inch size, were used to learn the rules of grammar. Still others were to be used as the basis for a book for new parents. It would encourage them to give not so much unusual names to their children, but rather names that had fallen from circulation. The cards reveal what I was reading back then: many of the names are those of actors and actresses, many were writers for the *New York Times*.

In sum the cards reveal a young man from Revere, Massachusetts moving up to where he knows what the TLS is, and what the NYRB is, but the truth is he also knows when he looks into the *Times Literary Supplement* and *The New York Review of Books* in the Bard College Library that he is – what? – a side or back door visitor, permitted a look-in on certain days, for a limited amount of time.

There is for me a thought, not always comforting (then and certainly now), that I am happy to plumb into the works of great writers and find my way, perhaps to a review of a new book on Philip Larkin, about whom I know a good deal and can savor or spit out most things written about him; something which may also be true of Alan Bennett, Penelope Fitzgerald, Elizabeth Bishop, Henry James, Virginia Woolf, and of course Janet Malcolm and Dwight Macdonald, Melville, Shaw, Camus and the three Johns – O'Hara, Cheever and Updike.

The box is now taped-up again and labeled, not to be reopened by me unless, possibly, when I am 90 and it is a rainy day and I am housebound. Or (more likely) I'll open the box when I have a need to go back and visit that young man. He will always be far from Revere, Massachusetts in space and time, someone who I am, at worst, able to laugh at, and at best someone that makes me proud, if not of the accomplishment, then certainly of the devoted-attempt to choose excellence. ▪

Holy Well

Eileen Favorite

When we traveled to northern Wisconsin for
vacation, we never wore seatbelts. We left the
windows wide open to the spice of weeds and
insecticide. I was usually stuck in the backseat
between my brothers, to keep them from fighting.
We'd pass gentle sloping fields of dairy cows,
magnificent red barns, silos of burnished steel.
I leaned forward, my chin on the front seat, and
watch the illusion of water on the hot road ahead.
We chased the apparent puddle, but never reached it.

I still feel the rub of vinyl under my chin, hear
the farm news my dad liked, as we moved toward
that ever-elusive slick puddle of oily sheen, that light
refracted, and which would disappear just as we
seemed only yards away. We could never splash our
tires in that water. We could never reach the holy well. **H**

Just Like Home

Scott Russell Morris

As we train through Italy for the first time, I tell
you how much it feels like home; or rather, how
it feels like Southern California, the place of my
childhood. You disagree, but I don't think you
know. The way the valleys move is the same, the
way the low hills wait in the background is the
same. Just like California: the khaki of the semi-dry
grass, the ripple of the distant trees, the rows of red
tile roofs, the muted consistency of the stucco walls.
Each building could be a holiday home and, this
close to the water, probably is. Of course, California
architecture was modeled on these very towns, but
California doesn't have so much hay, nor rows of
sunflowers. No castles sitting on the cliffs,

or cathedrals crowning the crest of each country
town. But still, the power lines are the same, their
catenaries identical as we speed past and I follow
their ups and downs with my fingers as I used to
while riding in the back seat of my parents' car
on I-15 into San Diego. You say only I would pay
attention to power lines on our first day in Italy.
You say they're the same everywhere. I suppose
they are. But if Mandelbrot is correct, when you
look closely enough every coastline is identical
and so are all the temperate valleys.
Yet here we are, hoping for – what? Something new?

H

The Fall

by Rebecca Stott

*L*ate summer, 1969. I'm five years old. At school everyone's talking about Neil Armstrong and the Moon landing, but I've got other things on my mind. I'm stashing food under my bed, stolen from the kitchen cupboard. There are several tins of corned beef down there, each with those little keys on the side that you have to twist to open. There are baked beans, packets of instant bolognese sauce and butterscotch-flavoured Angel Delight. I know it's not going to last us for long but it's a start. The Tribulations are coming any day now. I've heard my grandfather preach about them. First there'll be the Rapture and then the Tribulations and then Armageddon. The seas will rise and the stars will fall and the Four Horsemen will gallop across the rooftops of our street and all of Satan's people – that's all the people who are not in fellowship with us – will drown or burn or get buried alive. All our people, our parents and grandparents and uncles and aunts – that's the Exclusive Brethren, the good people – are going to go up in the Rapture before the bad things start, except for the not-good-enough ones who will get left behind. I'm pretty certain my brothers and I will get left behind, because we're not good enough. I'm not taking any chances. I'm going to be ready just in case.

Early spring, 2017. Almost fifty years later. It's school half term; the café in the Museum of London is busy. I take out my notebook and my favourite fountain pen. I'm wondering if I should record the interview. I'd recorded interviewees before, but it's usually awkward, too formal, not worth the trouble. It can put people on their guard. I decide to take notes instead.

'I haven't seen one of those in years,' Roy says, nodding at the pen and pulling up a seat opposite me at the café table. I pass him my pen. I show him how I fill it from the ink pot that I carry, screwing the pump system slowly one way and then the other to create a vacuum into which the ink pulls.

He's tall. He has large hands. He looks like the Curator of the Museum of London should look: smartly dressed, but his slightly scuffed boots and worn jeans suggest he'd be back in the soil of an archaeological dig in a heartbeat if someone handed him a shovel.

'Don't you worry about the glass breaking in your bag?' he asks, his eyes bright. 'All that ink spilling everywhere?'

'It's very thick glass,' I say.

But he's right. I probably should be more careful. I tell him about the things I've spilled in rucksacks over the years: the juice from the crab I bought in the fishmongers in Port Seton and the curry that leaked from a lunch box just before I was due to give a public lecture, leaving my notes and hands wet, warm and brick-red with turmeric stains.

We chat, but it's only a few minutes before I find my way to the girl, the Billingsgate Girl. It's already a kind of shorthand between us. A code.

She is why we are here.

'Would it be possible to talk to you about the Billingsgate Saxon brooch and the woman who wore it?' I'd written to him in an email a few weeks earlier. 'I'm doing some research.'

I'd described myself as a historian and a professor of literature, before adding that I was a novelist. Then I'd taken the word novelist out again, thinking he might think me frivolous, or worse: cavalier with facts. Then I'd put it back in. He could always find me on Google, after all, if he cared to check.

'Of course,' he'd replied. 'The brooch. Interesting. Not sure I can tell you anything you don't already know. But let's meet.'

I'd first seen the inch-or-so-wide brooch two years before, captured inside a simple, small frame hanging on the white wall of a corridor in the Museum of London. It had made the hairs on the back of my neck stand up.

The spotlit, empty corridor had been spooky enough. I'd just seen millions of artefacts in the Roman gallery behind me – coins, scraps of sandals, amulets, writing tablets, marble gods and pots – stuffed into glass cabinets. Then I'd stepped into that white corridor, empty save for a snaking timeline painted directly onto the wall and one tiny frame containing the brooch. While the other half-term visitors had rushed ahead to the Medieval gallery beyond, I had lingered to get my bearings. A sign on the wall explained that this corridor represented 'Dark Age' London. After the Romans left in AD 420, the ruined city had been abandoned by humans for four hundred years. If there were no humans inside the city walls, there were no artefacts to find, no stories to tell. Hence the blank, white corridor.

The number of objects that archaeologists have found inside the city walls during the derelict centuries of Londinium was so small, I read, that you could fit them inside a single shoebox; I was surprised that archaeologists used shoeboxes. The Billingsgate brooch was one of the objects in that 'shoebox'. That's why it was hanging here, now, in this otherwise empty corridor, this time hole. The

The number of objects that archaeologists have found inside the city walls during the derelict centuries of Londinium was so small ... that you could fit them inside a single shoebox

curators had framed the brooch beside another of similar design found in an early Anglo-Saxon grave in Mitcham, Surrey. If the two brooches had both been made in the same workshop, that dated them to around AD 450-500; and that meant someone must have dropped it around the same time. A woman. It was a woman's brooch. A Saxon woman had gone into the deserted, crumbling ruin of a city between AD 450-500. What was she doing there? What had made her drop her brooch?

The frame, hung at eye level, was about the size of the emergency button boxes you see on trains.

I stepped closer to get a better look. That's when the hairs on my neck started to stir. There was just me and the framed brooch in that empty corridor, my reflection passing across the glass between us. Everyone else had gone. The brooch felt like a talisman: magical and far away, yet intimate. Unsettling even under all that bright halogen lighting. There was something haunting about it. Or rather about the Saxon woman who must have worn it, a second-generation immigrant looting among the ruins.

Archaeologists, of course, knew nothing about her. How could they? She had long slipped away into all that dark earth. All they – we – knew was that she had walked across the fallen roof tiles of an abandoned Roman bathhouse and dropped her brooch. Soft, silty, dark soil had closed over it. And, except for the blind nuzzling of an occasional earthworm, mole or rat, the brooch had lain undisturbed for one thousand four hundred years, surfacing finally in 1968 when archaeologists found it amongst broken rooftiles and snail shells beneath the demolished Coal Exchange on Lower Thames Street. Now it was here, hanging on a wall in a corridor where no one stopped to look.

What I hadn't told Roy in my email then was that the Billingsgate Girl was already up and walking in my head, that I'd given her a name – Isla – and that I'd seen Isla in my mind's eye, more than once inside the ruined bathhouse within the ruined city. She'd become a kind of ghost. I could hear her sometimes even when I couldn't see her; scratching, foraging about, sometimes even muttering to herself. She was real. I could see her bare feet on those broken tiles, and once in a dream, she and I had together wrenched the door off an old Roman temple, only to be engulfed in a cloud of bats.

'I've brought the map,' I say to Roy, trying to shake the feeling that someone was walking over my grave. I unfold the latest version of the museum's map of the Roman city. It's brand new. I've just bought it in the gift shop to replace my worn-out copy. The thick paper crackles as I smooth out its fanned folds across the table. I put our coffee cups neatly back on top; there's nowhere else to put them. Roy nods with satisfaction, running his hand over the paper, peering in to admire the way the cartographer has superimposed the ruins of the Roman city – the forum right in the middle, the wharves along the waterfront, the grids of streets, amphitheatre, temples and fort – over modern London's grid of streets and landmarks.

I imagine Roy and me from above, as if we are in one of those scenes from a crime drama, where the detective and his assistant take a look at the map one last time and suddenly see something they haven't spotted before, something they'd missed.

'We know she dropped the brooch here,' I say, putting my finger on the site of the Billingsgate bathhouse on the north bank of the Thames. 'But how would she have actually got into the city? If her brooch was made in the same workshop as the brooch from Mitcham, let's say that's where she lived. If she walked up from Mitcham to the bridgehead here along the old Roman road Stane Street that's hours' walk.'

I'm showing off. I can't help it. I want him to know I've done the work.

'Walking distance?' he says.

I'd walked the whole route from Mitcham, following the line of the old Roman road, to find out how long it would have taken Isla, but I wasn't going to tell him that, at least not yet. I didn't want him to think me completely unhinged.

'Google maps,' I say. I'd also measured the distance and checked the walking time.

'If she came up Stane Street through Southwark,' he says, running his finger over the line where the road once crossed between the islands south of the river, 'she'd be walking through abandoned Roman industrial sites. All along here there were smithies.' He smiles. 'Good places to scavenge.'

For iron my Isla will risk the ghosts, wolves, rats and vengeful gods of an abandoned city

In my mind's eye she's carrying a wicker basket on her back, to carry the nails, coins, door hinges, spoons, knives and brooches that she's intending to dig out of the ruins. Iron is scarce. For iron my Isla will risk the ghosts, wolves, rats and vengeful gods of an abandoned city. She's a looter. She must be a looter.

We both look back down at the map, conjuring different ruinous scenarios for that road stretching ahead of us; from the wattle and daub buildings of the small Anglo-Saxon settlement behind, towards the ruined stone city walls that we can just see on the horizon, beyond a stretch of brown river. As if we've gone from Google Aerial View to Street View in a single click. Now we are standing side by side on a straight road, looking around at derelict forges and workshops to either side, plants pushing up through cracks, ruined carts and old chariots rotting and rusting by the verge.

'If she came to the city by boat,' I say, now that I've got myself along the Roman road and right to the river's edge, 'I mean if she had access to a boat on the south bank, she could have moored up on the north side here where the Roman harbours were, just a few hundred feet from the bathhouse.' I run my fingers along the map to the north foreshore in front of the Billingsgate site.

She's in a rowing boat, pulling across choppy steel grey water towards the wild ruin of stone and rubble and trees ahead. My pulse quickens with the courage of the girl, the sense of danger and excitement she must have felt. I can see the wet revetements rising above her, the winches and pullies of the old Roman harbour black and wet against a lowering sky.

'Saxon boats were shallow draft,' he says. 'They needed beaches to pull their boats onto. That's why they settled over near the Strand where the riverbank is flat and shingly.'

The boat Isla's rowing in my mind, I realise now, is just like the ones I used to row in the rowing club I'd joined in my forties: wooden, with neat brass holders for the oars, a seat in the middle that slides up and down. I've never rowed a flat-bottomed boat. I don't even know what a Saxon boat would look like, let alone how it might handle on open water.

'But she could still have tied it to one of the jetties over there, couldn't she?' My finger is on the north waterfront just in front of the bathhouse.

'Most of the Roman jetties would have rotted by AD 500,' he says. 'By the time your girl arrived, all along here would have been just a mess of rotting timber and silt.'

Did he just say 'your girl'?

No wellington boots, I'm thinking, watching her climb out and onto the slippery jetty. Leather sandals if she was lucky, or just bare feet. What if you got a piece of iron in your foot, or a slither of wood? It would soon get infected. They didn't have antibiotics.

She is my girl, yes. She's mine. And now she's got a nasty gash on her foot.

I'd seen that foot before, white against the rust red of fallen and cracked Roman roof tiles. I look at it again now – it's my daughter's foot, fully-grown to adult size but with toes shaped like a toddler's and mottled with chilblains. Soft and pink. I try to put a sandal on the foot – it's cold – but then realise I can't remember what early Anglo-Saxon sandals look like. It's cold and that gash is bleeding and it's covered in mud.

I'm suddenly overwhelmed by this darkest of all dark corners of the Dark Ages. I look back at the map for something solid, a clue. If she came from the south, she must have crossed the river. If the wharves were rotten and slippery and her boat too shallow to moor easily, how else would she have got in? Then I see the line of the Roman bridge spanning the water. The Billingsgate bathhouse is only a stone's throw from the bridgehead on the north-bank. Could Isla have walked across that bridge, crossed the river that way? Could the bridge still have been standing in AD 500?

And the Thames ... would have been much wider then than it was now. Humans have narrowed its channel through a thousand years of waterfront infilling and building

I'd always imagined that first bridge of Londinium thick with people, mules and carts, just as it is in the tiny model in the museum gallery. On first seeing it I'd recalled the line in T.S. Eliot's The Wasteland, where he imagines the dead crossing the river and writes: 'I had not thought death had undone so many'. But the bridge my Isla would have seen from the south bank would surely have been a precarious wooden structure, just a few stumps bearing planks here and there and the great rush of water underneath. And the Thames, I remind myself, would have been much wider then than it is now. Humans have narrowed its channel through a thousand years of waterfront infilling and building.

'Silly question,' I say, 'but how long might the bridge have stood after the Romans left?'

He doesn't laugh at me. He's taking me seriously. These are not stupid questions. They interest him. He has started slipping back into the present tense. We both have. Sometimes we correct ourselves. Sometimes we don't.

'We don't know,' he says. 'It's probably down by then or at least partially down. But maybe not. Roman river bridges were built to last. There's bits of them still standing all over the world.'

'OK,' I say, treading carefully, 'so could she have walked across?' I had lowered my voice. Why had I done that? My face is flushed too, but not from embarrassment. It's like she's here. Like she's watching.

'It's impossible to say,' he admits. He has lowered his voice too, but he's not mocking me. His brow is furrowed. 'Pretty unlikely, I'd say.'

'Why don't you know?' I want to ask. 'How can you not know?' His not-knowing is unsettling me.

Isla's making her way across the river, on a patched-together, ramshackle wooden structure, towards the ruins on the other side. She has to crawl sometimes. Her tunic is billowing out in a cross wind. She's hungry. She pulls a crust of bread from a pocket in her tunic. She looks out across the water and gathers her cloak around her.

'I read somewhere,' I say, 'that the number of objects you've found in the layers of the derelict city, you could fit into a single shoe box? Is that true?'

'It is. Amazing isn't it?'

'Is it still true? I mean surely they must have found more things in the Crossrail excavations?'

'Most of the objects they've found so far belong to early Londinium, not late. So, yes, it's still a shoebox only about half full: a belt buckle or two, the brooch, some bits of pottery imported from Gaza.'

'So the people living in and around the derelict city didn't go in at all?'

'Or we just haven't found them yet.'

'But why didn't they?'

'Why would they?'

We both know that's a stupid question. Why didn't they go in? Because the ruined city would have been dangerous, fetid, full of rubbish, fallen buildings and wild animals. Both the local people and the Anglo-Saxon immigrants would have needed land to grow their crops and to pen their livestock. They needed fresh water, timber from trees. If you'd been part of a first-generation Anglo-Saxon family, newly arrived, you'd have chosen a settlement site with half-decent soil somewhere near a Roman road, with a forest for your building materials and firewood, and close to a river for water and a shingly beach to pull up your boat. You'd take the land that wasn't already being farmed by locals; the unclaimed bits. You might have cut a clearing in the forest here, or a bit of marshland there. You wouldn't be interested in ruins. You wouldn't have time.

'But I'd have gone in,' I want to say. 'I would have gone in there.' And I'm pretty certain by now that if Roy had been an Anglo-Saxon man living in the hinterland of the ruined city, he'd have gone in too. If you saw those great ruins looming up on the horizon, red at sunset, gold at dawn, whilst you were ploughing or herding cows, all that great span of stone riverbank wall reflected in the river, gates wide open, how could you not want to go and poke around in there? Especially if your people only ever built small clusters of huts out of timber and you'd never seen buildings made of stone before. And even if curiosity wasn't enough to take you over the water and in through the gates, you might go to scavenge for Roman metalwork, or for pots and stone, because once the Romans had gone you had to make do and mend. There was no currency any more, very few imports, probably no market places. And, for at least two generations after the Romans left, if your cooking pot broke there were no potters to craft you a new one. You'd have to go and forage in the Roman cemetery to get yourself a funerary urn if you wanted to make your tea.

Isla has crossed the bridge, or moored her boat, and now she's following high walkways over the brackish mud and across rooftops. She's looking down on young oak and birch trees pushing up through cracked mosaic floors and fallen masonry. Statues of Roman emperors and gods lie broken and dismembered between rubbish heaps where wild boars, dogs and rats scavenge. She sees crows roosting in the ceilings of great villas; geese and swans drifting on green ponds formed in the pools of a colonnaded bathhouse.

'But if Isla is looting,' I say and catch myself, switching back to past tense quickly, 'If she was looting, she wouldn't have been the only one. I mean if it was worth her while to go into the city, it must have been worth it for others too.'

'Yes, true. Isla?'

'The girl,' I say, looking away. 'A nickname.'

'Funny. We're not supposed to give names to the bodies we find,' he says. 'Just a number. We have to stay neutral. It's hard to resist sometimes though. You make attachments.'

'Of course,' I say. 'How can you not imagine scenarios and real people – to fill in the gaps, I mean?'

Now I'm seeing the images of the hooded looters I'd seen in television footage of the Tottenham riots. The looters had all been men. They carried flatscreen TVs still in their boxes. Some of them had used shopping trolleys. They'd seemed to approach the task in an organized way, in groups; one watching the street, another holding the trolley, the rest climbing in through the broken glass of shop windows. Would Isla have looted as part of a pack? One watching out, one with a wooden handcart, the others climbing into the empty buildings, digging about? They could never have got a handcart back across that broken-down bridge, and certainly not loaded with loot. They'd have had to carry it, on their backs perhaps, in wicker baskets. Perhaps Isla came in by boat because she could ferry more out.

The looters had all been men. They carried flatscreen TVs still in their boxes. Some of them had used shopping trolleys

Sometime between dusk and dawn in that bathhouse Isla dropped one of the two matching bronze brooches that held her tunic together, where the cloth folded between her shoulder sockets and her collar bone. Her tunic might have come loose, flapping in the night wind. Perhaps she roughly knotted the ends together to hold it up as she scrambled in the darkness to find her brooch. Maybe there was someone else in there with her – friend or foe?

And, after she had stumbled home with her loot or, worse, crawled off bruised and violated, over time the dark earth and silt closed over the fallen bathhouse where she had walked, covering its roof tiles, mosaics and the broken limbs of Roman statues, dark earth made up of a slow compost of weeds, thatch, leaves, the bodies of thousands of dead worms, insects and small mammals.

'You said "research,"' Roy says, 'but you didn't say what.'

What happens when there's no high street and no Amazon and no central heating, no refuse collections?

Neither of us have talked about the news. Neither of us has mentioned Brexit or the Paris climate talks. I want to ask him if he's ever thought about what it is going to be like when the electricity runs out, when the food shortages and droughts force climate refugees north in their millions. What happens when there's no high street and no Amazon and no central heating, no refuse collections? What will we do when the rivers rise and flood the railway lines?

Only a week before, sleepless, I'd checked the interactive map I'd found online to see where the river would flood near my house in Norwich. I'd clicked on the two-degree temperature rise scenario and seen the River Yare, all reedbeds and swans, spill its banks over its flood plain, engulfing the railway line and station, and the cathedral right up to its flying buttresses, but not my house. Then I'd clicked on the four-degree temperature rise and watched the river water rise further again, up to the road just below my home. Even with a four-degree rise, my house, built on a hill, was just above the flood plain. I'd exhaled, thinking of the new view from my kitchen window, swans nesting on chimney pots poking up through the swollen river. Below the water line, there'd be submerged houses, furniture, keepsakes, old photographs floating about in abandoned rooms.

I'd made the mistake of telling a friend what I'd found out. Then, when she'd asked anxiously if her street would be OK, and how long this was all going to take, I realized I hadn't checked. I could see there were some things that were probably best not talked about amongst friends.

'Research – I don't know yet,' I say to Roy. 'It won't show its face.'

Now I've done it. It won't show its face. What did I mean by that odd phrase? Now he was definitely going to think me unhinged.

I cough. Then I say. 'Sometimes it's like that for a while. With fiction I mean. Sometimes with non-fiction too.'

'Early days,' he nods.

'I keep hitting brick walls,' I say. I want to understand. I want to explain. I'm thinking of the girl with the baked beans and corned beef and Angel Delight sachets stashed under the bed. She'd

have made a fine looter. 'I can't tell if it's just me,'
I say, 'or or if I'm missing something. Some days
I think it's collapsing empires that I'm interested
in; sometimes it's what happens to people when
infrastructures collapse; sometimes it's the girl.
Usually it's just the girl.'

'Isla.'

'I'd give anything to walk through Londinium
a hundred years after the Romans left. Then a
hundred and fifty. Then two hundred. What would
it have looked like without any humans?'

**After thirty years without humans, the species in
there are exploding: wolves, dogs, bears, geese, red
kites. Seems humans are more dangerous to other
species than radiation**

'I think about that a lot,' he says.

He opens his laptop and pulls up a file on his
computer with hundreds of photographs of derelict
modern cities he's collected from books and from the
internet. Hundreds. He scrolls through close-ups of
trees pushing up through cracks in concrete, wolves
in churches, birds nesting in rusting filing cabinets.

No wonder, I think, no wonder we both keep
slipping into the present tense.

'You have to go to a city like Pripyat, I reckon,'
he says, 'if you want to know what Londinium
looked like.'

'Pripyat?'

'The city that got sealed off after the Chernobyl
disaster. After thirty years without humans, the
species in there are exploding: wolves, dogs, bears,

geese, red kites. Seems humans are more dangerous to other species than radiation. Species come back and flourish once people are out of the way.'

'That's good,' I say. 'Maybe the planet should just shake us off.'

I think I understand what Isla is. She isn't persistence after the apocalypse. She isn't even survival after a climate catastrophe. Isla is a pair of eyes, a lone human in a post-human city, where traces of human life are slowly disappearing forever. She's a witness. **H**

BLUE MURDER

by Ian Thomson

Daniel Morgan, one of Britain's 10,000-odd registered private detectives, was reckoned to be an ace surveillance man. On the night of 10th March 1987, however, he was murdered on leaving the Golden Lion public house, Sydenham Road, south-east London. He had been drinking with his business partner Jonathan Rees. A customer discovered the body in the pub car park at about 9.40pm. An axe was embedded in his face.

Three blows had been delivered with the blade to the back of the detective's head followed by a final blow to the side. On the blood-puddled asphalt were the keys to his silver BMW coupé and two unopened packets of crisps. Morgan, 37, a brawny, mustachioed man, lived in South Norwood with his wife Iris and their two children, Sarah and Daniel. Were he alive now he would be 71.

Three decades on, Morgan's killer remains unidentified and the circumstances surrounding his death are ever more murky. With rumours of sexual jealousy, tabloid newspaper corruption and Scotland Yard wrongdoing, 'The Golden Wonder' murder – named for the crisps found at the crime scene – has become the most-investigated unsolved killing in British history.

Preliminary enquiries established that the murder weapon was a £45 Chinese-manufacture Diamond Brand chopping axe. Round the handle were two strips of sticking plaster, either these were to afford a better grip or to ensure that no fingerprints remained. Morgan's £830 Rolex wrist watch had been stolen – but £1100 left untouched in a jacket pocket. Robbery thus seemed an unlikely motive. A contract hit? Certainly as a qualified bailiff Morgan had made enemies; he specialised in debt collection and vehicle seizure; he snooped on errant spouses and undertook other sorry gumshoe work. The banknotes were most likely part of an outstanding payment to the detective agency he had set up with Jonathan Rees in Thornton Heath, south-west London, in 1984: Southern Investigations.

Like many detective agencies, Southern Investigations was comfortably flexible in its attitude to the law. Morgan himself had an illegal link into the Police National Computer, but his colleague Rees operated at a much more sleazy end of the trade. A big, bluff northerner from Rotherham in South Yorkshire, on the sly Rees made money from selling confidential information to the 'redtop' nationals. During the 1990s, Rupert Murdoch's *News of the World* paid him in excess of £150,000 a year for information on, among other notables, Prince Edward and the Countess of Wessex (whose bank accounts he infiltrated), Peter Mandelson, Gary Lineker, Mick Jagger and Eric Clapton. As a freemason with police associates, Rees was very much part of a Thatcher-era story of press intrusion, public sector corruption and criminality. In those days, especially in London south of the river, police and thieves were not infrequently one and the same. While Rees was pleased to dine with Met officers at Masonic events in Croydon, Morgan had a low opinion of the police. 'All police are bastards!' he was heard to say shortly before his death.

Born in colonial Singapore in 1949 to an army officer father, Morgan was a hard-working, self-reliant man with a memory for car number plates and other potentially incriminating detail. 'He knew the *Guinness Book of Records* back to front', his brother Alastair would recall. It was nothing for Morgan to drive from London to the West Country and back in a single day's sleuthing. However, relations had soured between Morgan and Rees. Morgan complained to Alastair that he was doing all the agency's work while Rees lounged in pubs with his masonic 'bent copper' mates.

At the time of his murder, Morgan was romantically involved with Margaret Harrison, a Thornton Heath estate agent with two teenage daughters. There is some suggestion that Harrison may also have been involved with Rees. Allegedly, Rees paid for her daughters' school fees, and was often on the phone to her. Harrison later told an inquest that she had been on a date with Rees on the day of the murder, but insisted that she slept only with Morgan. She was unable to explain the sixty or so calls Rees had made to her from his car-phone in the three months prior to the murder. One of these had lasted twelve minutes. Rees's wife Sharon was later at a loss

– or perhaps unwilling – to corroborate his claim that the call was made by her, not by him, and concerned a takeaway Indian meal. (They subsequently divorced.)

At 8.00pm on the evening of 9th March, the day before his murder, Morgan met Rees and a police officer friend of his in the Golden Lion, a pub he did not usually frequent. He parked his BMW on the street outside, and went in to find Detective Sergeant Sid Fillery of Catford C.I.D.

Fillery, a serving officer of 23 years (and, like Rees, a freemason), was at that time working illegally as a security guard for Rees at a car auctions business in Charlton south of the Thames. The previous year, on the evening of 6th March 1986, Rees claimed to have been mugged of £18,000 in Belmont Car Auctions takings, sprayed with ammonia and coshed after failing to deposit the cash in a Midland Bank nightsafe (which, he insisted, had been 'superglued' shut). Morgan did not believe him. He was certain that Rees had faked the robbery and pocketed the money for himself and Fillery. Whether from sexual envy or some other friction within the partnership, relations between Morgan and Rees had since 'turned to hatred', according to their bookkeeper, Kevin Lennon.

As the evening progressed, a row erupted after Morgan was overheard to shout that he was opposed to hiring officers of Fillery's sort because they reflected badly on Southern Investigations. Fillery retaliated that he did not care for Morgan's appearance, his garrulousness or his flirtatious way with women. He ought to mind his fucking step. After the quarrel, the men drank on together in silence. Morgan agreed to meet Rees in the same pub the following day in order to resume the argument and (it later emerged) to meet Paul Goodridge, a former showbiz bodyguard in the pay of Liz Taylor and Bo Derek.

Morgan's last moments can be pieced together only sketchily. At 6.30pm on 10th March he briefly met his mistress Margaret Harrison at Regan's Wine Bar on Brigstock Road, Thornton Heath. Harrison would later recall that Morgan appeared to be his 'normal self' as they chatted over a bottle of wine. She and Morgan had been in a 'loose relationship' for eighteen months. Some time after 7.00pm, Morgan left Harrison so as to meet Rees at the Golden Lion. For some reason he parked his car in the secluded, poorly lit car park round the back of the pub.

There were few customers in the Golden Lion that night. After arguing again with Morgan about the car auction 'robbery', Rees departed at 8.55 pm, leaving Morgan to complete some agency paperwork. Goodridge never did turn up. At about 9.15pm Morgan walked through the beer garden to the rear of the pub, where someone was waiting for him. Joseph O'Brien, the publican, was alerted by a customer: 'Joe, I think there's a body… or a dummy out in the car park.' A smartly dressed drunk appeared to have collapsed beside a parked BMW. O'Brien instantly telephoned for the police and within minutes a squad car arrived, followed by an ambulance.

Sid Fillery of the Catford plainclothes squad was assigned to the case. He interviewed Rees under caution and accompanied him to the mortuary in order to identify the body. Fillery also took possession of documents from Southern Investigations (among them, Morgan's diary for that year of 1987), but initially failed to disclose to his police superiors that he was moonlighting for the Thornton Heath-based agency or that he and Rees were close friends. So the first investigation was corrupted – the Met subsequently admitted as much – by the actions of Detective Sergeant

> **So the first investigation was corrupted – the Met subsequently admitted as much – by the actions of Detective Sergeant Fillery**

Fillery. A month later, Fillery and two other Catford officers were arrested and questioned on suspicion of perverting the course of justice. Rees and his brothers-in-law Glenn and Gary Vian, part-time security bouncers involved in south London drug trade trafficking, were also arrested – on suspicion of murder. Following eighteen hours of interrogation, all six men were released without charge.

During the coroner's inquest held a year later, in April 1988, it was suggested by Julian Nutter, the lawyer representing Rees, that the Golden Lion was a pub frequented by a local drugs dealer.

'The dealer was known to use a minder who had a frightening tool of the trade – an axe.' Nutter speculated that Morgan had been killed after stumbling on – or interfering with – a drugs transaction. The inquest, conducted by Sir Montague 'Monty' Levine, again raised concerns of police collusion. Kevin Lennon, the bookkeeper, testified that Rees and his Catford Met contacts had arranged a £1000 contract for Morgan's murder. ('I've got it fixed', Rees reportedly told Lennon six months before the murder.) The killing was to be staged within the jurisdiction of Catford; that way, the officers involved could suppress damaging evidence linking them.

Incredibly, not one strand of forensic evidence was found to implicate anyone. 'No blood. No fibres. No fingerprints', said the coroner, who returned a verdict of unlawful killing. Four months after the inquest, in August 1988, Morgan was buried in Beckenham cemetery in a 'recuperable' coffin: cremation was not an option in case the body had to be exhumed for further forensic testing. In police parlance, even at this early stage, the Morgan case was a 'sticker' – one that would not be solved.

It seems likely that Morgan was about to expose a case of extensive drug-related police corruption implicating Rees, Fillery and other South London Met officers. Understandably Morgan did not trust the police to investigate; he himself had influential press contacts (among them, Alastair Campbell at the *Mirror*) and might eventually have decided to sell his story to the *News of the World*. In the late 1980s, after Fillery had brazenly joined Southern Investigations as Rees's replacement partner, the Morgan family began to speak openly of a police cover-up. The detective's mother , Isobel Hulsmann, claimed that 'Daniel had vital information – he had to be silenced.'

During a third police enquiry, launched covertly in 1998, the Southern Investigations office was bugged. No evidence that Rees was involved in Morgan's murder was recorded, but the listening device picked up on a conspiracy hatched by Rees to plant Class A drugs on a woman in a child custody case. Also exposed was Rees's involvement in Fleet Street corruption. A contact at the *Sunday Mirror* had asked Rees to access the bank accounts of Prince Edward and the Countess of Wessex.

Reporter: Do you remember a couple of months ago, you got me some details on Edward's business and Sophie's businesses and how well they were doing?

Rees: Yeah.

Reporter: And you did a check on Sophie's bank account?

Rees: Yeah.

Reporter: Is it possible to do that again? I'm not exactly sure what they're after but they seem to be under the impression that, you know, she was in the paper the other day for appearing in *Hello* magazine. They think she's had some kind of payment off them.

Rees: What? Off of *Hello*?

Reporter: Um, yeah.

Rees: … find out how much.

Reporter: Well, we just want to see if there's been any change to her bank account.

Rees was arrested and sentenced to seven years imprisonment for perverting the course of justice. Daniel Morgan's former colleague was at last behind bars – but not for his murder.
The heat was closing in all the same.

—

On 26th June 2002, Morgan's mother appeared on the BBC television programme Crimewatch. Isobel Hulsmann's emotional appeal was accompanied by a police reward of £50,000 for information.
'How could I have had my son taken away from me like this? What sort of people do this?… It's cruel, it's evil, it's awful. Daniel harmed nobody.' By now, the campaign for justice for her son had gone on for fifteen years. 'I can't move on. I want to move on so desperately. I shall soon be 75 and I just would love to have a few years of peace of mind.'
Detective Chief Superintendent David Cook, a courteous, dry-humoured Scot, led the fourth inquiry. I was covering the case for the *Independent* newspaper; Cook was interviewed by me shortly after the Crimewatch episode had aired, on 18th September 2002, at Hendon police headquarters,

Aerodrome Road, north-west London. He told me: 'This is a tremendously interesting story. Interesting beyond belief. Any investigation into Morgan's death has to begin with the near-certainty that it was a conspiracy and not the work of a lone individual. Not all those involved may have known that Morgan was going to be killed, but they certainly knew that something was going to happen.'

One of the many rumours related to Morgan is that he was killed by a woman: the Elastoplast round the axe handle was said to indicate the grip of small hands

It was imperative that Morgan's murder be solved: not only was the Met's honour at stake, said Cook, but the dead man's family was owed 'long wished-for peace of mind.' Cook went on to say that he had been 'delighted' with the Crimewatch response and believed that he had found a 'nugget – but whether it's a 24-carat nugget, we'll have to see.'

One of the many rumours related to Morgan is that he was killed by a woman: the Elastoplast round the axe handle was said to indicate the grip of small hands. Cook said with finality: 'No. In my view, Morgan was not killed by a woman.... But yes, passion comes from many sources. Greed – financial greed – encourages passion. And this is a story about greed – greed pure and simple.'

'Margaret Harrison?'

'We've spoken to Morgan's mistress. The fact that she was with Morgan just two hours prior to his murder means that she's inevitably part of our investigation. I mean: to say that she's *not* involved in the investigation would be wrong. However, we've no reason to believe that she's a suspect.'

'Could Rees have left the Golden Lion in the knowledge that Morgan was about to be killed?'

'I'm not prepared to say "yes" or "no". But it tells us something about Rees's character, doesn't it, that he planted drugs on an innocent woman so that her husband could get access to their child. He's not the sort of person I'd have round to tea.'

I asked about Paul Goodridge, the showbiz minder.

'Goodridge is part of the whole… shadow behind the Morgan mystery. I'm not just looking at the people I think are responsible. I'm looking at the people who *surrounded* the people I think are responsible.'

Cook had taken the investigation abroad.

'Enquiries have been made in Denmark – Morgan used to live in Denmark, he had a Danish girlfriend there in his student days. And we've also been to Malta. He did a car repossession job there – a "motor snatch-back" – shortly before his death.'

'And Sid Fillery. What about Sid Fillery?'

'To be honest with you, I'd have more chance of knowing the truth about Fillery's activities in the Force than I would in giving you the lottery numbers. Shadowy is not the word for him.'

'Morgan's missing Rolex is odd, isn't it?'

'Well, it's one of the many mysteries in the Morgan case. The watch hasn't been traced. Rolexes are unique – each with its own serial number – so they're pretty hard to get rid of.'

'Maybe there was an inscription on the back? An incriminating inscription?'

'Maybe, odds are we'll never know.'

Cook believed that he had identified the getaway car – a pale green VW Polo – but much about the case remained obscure.

'Some things might even have been deliberately obscured – still, I'm getting a pretty good picture now and my determination to catch the sods responsible is strong. I've got officers all over the place. I've got things happening.'

Or so Cook thought. Unknown to him, the *News of the World* had put him and his wife, Jacqui Hames, under surveillance. Two hired vans followed Cook as he took his two-year-old son to nursery. Why? At the 2011-2012 Leveson press inquiry Hames, herself a Crimewatch presenter, rejected as 'absolutely pathetic' the claim made by the newspaper's then editor Rebekah Brooks that her journalists were 'investigating whether Jacqui Hames was conducting an affair with David Cook'.

It is much more likely that suspects in the Morgan murder were using the *News of the World* to intimidate the family and 'subvert the investigation.' Eight years later, the Cook-Hames marriage dissolved owing perhaps to the stress caused by press intrusion and surveillance. Meanwhile Sid Fillery, who had been running Southern Investigations while Rees was in jail, was arrested in April 2003 when anti-corruption officers found evidence on his personal computer of child pornography. He was charged and convicted. Detective Cook, as yet unaware of the tabloid surveillance, had meanwhile persuaded south

London career criminals, relatives and enemies to turn Queen's evidence and talk about the Morgan murder. In return, they were offered reduced sentences, protection and new identities.

The Old Bailey trial began in September 2009. Legal arguments went on for eighteen months – the longest pre-trial wrangling in British judicial history – until the trial collapsed in March 2011 after three 'supergrass' witnesses were discredited and the Met claimed to have lost track of documents relative to the case. The prosecution alleged that Morgan was murdered after he discovered that Rees was using Southern Investigations to launder the proceeds from drug trafficking. Rees's brother-in-law Glenn Vian had reportedly wielded the axe; Glenn's brother Gary had acted as look-out. Rees was the bait to get Morgan into the pub; Jimmy Cook, an associate, was the getaway man. Sid Fillery, having himself been accused of perverting the course of justice, joined the four others and left the Old Bailey a free man.

With the collapse of the Old Bailey hearing, those who murdered Morgan will most likely never be brought to book. Nevertheless, the then Home Secretary Theresa May, disquieted by what she called this 'horrific murder', opened a Hillsborough-style independent inquiry in the spring of 2013. Police promised to co-operate but for the first two years they hesitated to hand over any incriminating case papers. Nothing came of the inquiry. So far the Morgan case has cost the British taxpayer over £50 million in police and other expenditures. There is more than enough darkness in this murder for us all; the Home Office has in fact promised to review the case in 2019.

And now? Southern Investigations is defunct. Sid Fillery helps to run a pub in Great Yarmouth, Norfolk; Jonathan Rees lives with his mistress Margaret Harrison in Weybridge, Surrey. The *News of the World*, after 168 years in print, closed down in 2011 following revelations of phone hacking in which Rees was implicated. The Golden Lion, a former Victorian music-hall, has been refurbished many times with chintz fittings, brass candlesticks and framed sepia photographs. The pale peach ceiling is new but otherwise the Golden Lion remains every inch a south-east London community pub. The only shadow cast across the interior is the killing, on the night of 10th March 1987, of the detective who knew too much. H

A Hostess
of the
Floating World

水商売

by Susan Karen Burton

Sarah[1] was introduced to hostessing by a Japanese woman who lived in the room next to hers at a gaijin house, a hostel for foreigners. Sarah had arrived in Japan as an exchange student but fell so in love with Tokyo life – the delicate cuisine, the politeness of the people, the cloudless skies on warm autumn days – that she dropped out and stayed on. In need of a job, she was taken by her Japanese neighbour to meet the owner of a little snack bar in Ginza.

Ginza is an upmarket district of Tokyo known for its expensive department stores, designer boutiques and Michelin-starred restaurants. It is a ten-minute walk from the financial district of Marunouchi and the Imperial Palace. The bar was located near the shinkansen (bullet train) tracks in a grid network of streets filled with sushi bars, ramen noodle shops, shabu shabu restaurants and art galleries. Despite the worn red carpet and the patched black seats, the bar was cosy and inviting. A cluttered counter could sit ten customers huddled together and two low tables could accommodate ten more. The walls were lined with glass cabinets crammed with whisky bottles, Japanese brands such as Yamazaki and Hibiki, and the occasional cognac. Above them were pinned the autographs of famous customers:

1. Some names and places have been changed.

sumo wrestlers, football players and even a famous rakugo performer. The mama-san, in her fifties, was an ex-hostess who had opened her own place, as ex-hostesses sometimes do. Always immaculately dressed in a kimono that reflected the season, on any given night she was assisted by three Japanese girls in their early twenties. The mama-san looked the young foreigner over and invited her to try out at the bar for a few months. Sarah worked there for thirteen years. The dress code at the bar was formal, either short cocktail dresses with beading and sequins or long ball gowns with frills and chiffon. Although they had to look expensive, these confections could be bought for 3000 Yen (around 26 US dollars) in the underground shops near Shibuya and Shinjuku train stations, and in the bargain basements of department stores.

The customers, mostly high-ranking executives and company bosses in their fifties and sixties were, Sarah recalls, 'gentlemen types.' When moving jobs, a hostess's worth can be calculated by how many customers she can persuade to move with her to her new place of business. Most of the snack bar customers had been loyal clients of the mama-san in her younger days and they came to the bar primarily to see her.

The bar opened at 7.30pm. When customers came through the door, Sarah would take their coats, seat them and mix their drinks. In Japan, regular patrons buy their own bottles of liquor that are kept for them behind the bar (a custom known as 'bottle keep') and brought out on each visit.

Older Japanese men drink mizuwari, whisky and water, so Sarah would often mix this with chunks of ice. If the customer requested snacks, Sarah would bring small plates of mixed nuts, cheese and crackers, or chocolate. If they went to the toilet, she would hand them an oshibori, a hot hand towel, on their return.

To learn the correct polite behaviour, Sarah copied the other girls. Hostesses must never cross their legs, but should sit with their knees together at all times. Drinks, snacks and oshibori must always be offered with two hands and a slight bow. And if the customer takes out a packet of cigarettes the hostess must have a lighter ready for his Lark Black Label or Mild Seven Light. Smoking is permitted in public places in Japan, and the air in the bar was always gritty with cigarette smoke. When the hostesses did their end-of-year cleaning, they had to wipe down walls sticky with tar.

Whilst a geisha is an expert in singing and dancing, a hostess is a gei-no-nai geisha, a no-talent geisha. Her expertise lies in one area: conversation. When Sarah was introduced to a customer, he would present his meishi (business card), and Sarah would make small talk about his job, the news, the weather or some celebrity gossip, anything to help him forget about his work day or his sometimes-difficult home life. Customers must always be flattered and praised: for their business achievements, their singing, their ties. Customers who wanted to show off their fluency in the English language might regale Sarah with stories of their business trips to London. Some only wanted to talk to the mama-san, or to drink alone. Then Sarah would sit quietly, periodically refilling their glasses. Hostess clubs make their money not from the girls but from the sale of alcohol. A hostess's job is to encourage customers to relax, to stay longer and to drink more.

Flirting and lewd talk is generally considered acceptable in hostess bars, as it is in any environment where alcohol is consumed. Touching hostesses is not acceptable, but a wandering hand can always be blamed on a state of inebriation. Sex is not a feature of the hostess's job, though this does not always deter a customer from suggesting it. Recalls Sarah, 'Half of it is semi-joking but still it's like, "How about we go to a hotel? I promise I'll be quick".' Sarah would always answer, 'Please ask the mama because she is our manager,' and then watch as the mama-san threw them out. It is no accident that hostess bars are presided over by women known as 'mamas'. The mama-san is a matriarchal figure who allows company titans to indulge in infantile behaviour while protecting her hostesses and the reputation of her establishment.

Demonstrating subservience to male customers is part of the hostess's job; seemingly an odd one for a liberated foreign woman. But for Sarah a change of language could affect a switch in cultural identity and thus her attitude towards the customer.

'If I was talking to a customer in Japanese then my mind would go into Japanese mode and it wouldn't be me, and so I found it easier to act all womanly, the way they would want me to act,' she explains. 'But if I was talking to a customer who wanted to speak in English I would be in English woman mode so would get really annoyed if they made any sexist or sleazy comments.'

Karaoke (literally, 'empty orchestra') is a serious pastime in Japan and a staple of Japanese hostess clubs. At the little Ginza snack bar, the customer would choose a song from a catalogue and Sarah would punch the track's number into a console

Hostesses were warned not to dominate the karaoke machine – it is for the customers' use not the hostesses' – but Sarah was often asked to sing for patrons

at the table. When the first notes rang out, the customer would be handed a microphone and could sing hitokara (alone) or in a duet. An accomplished singer, Sarah was a popular duet partner and she learned a wide range of Japanese songs so that she could accompany customers. Hostesses were warned not to dominate the karaoke machine – it is for the customers' use not the hostesses' – but Sarah was often asked to sing for patrons, forlorn ballads such as the Okinawan song Subete no hito no kokoro ni hana O (Flowers for your Heart), saccharine-tinged folk songs such as Nagori Yuki (Fallen Snow), and always, always, the theme song from Titanic.

Hostessing at the little Ginza snack bar was, reminisces Sarah, an easy and enjoyable job. She got along well with the other girls and even introduced several of her own friends to the work. 'It was a really nice atmosphere, very friendly,' she says. Sarah worked at the bar three nights a week and went home with 10,000 Yen (around 90 US dollars) per night for four hours work.

Sarah's smooth vocals occasionally carried her through the neon city to Roppongi, Tokyo's most internationalised district. Here, the residents of high-rise apartments and international hotels gaze down onto a maze of pubs, strip joints and cabarets, some of which have connections with the Yakuza, the Japanese mafia. At an exclusive gentlemen's club, members paid a 50,000 Yen (around 447 US dollars) entrance fee to be welcomed by bowing doormen into a luxurious lounge with deep carpets, velvet sofas, bookcases and an open fire. A younger clientele, generally men in their thirties, talked, drank and danced with a collection of exquisitely beautiful Japanese girls who could match them for ambition and business acumen. For these girls hostessing was a highly lucrative but short-term career. Every evening before coming to work they paid 3000 Yen (around 26 US dollars) to have their hair professionally dressed in the Roppongi style, more flamboyant than in other hostessing districts, with greater volume, tighter curls and clouds of glitter hairspray. And they read the hostess's bible, Koakuma Ageha magazine, to keep abreast of hostess club fashions including famous hostess's own-brand products, make-up and accessories. They were 'very, very ambitious girls,' remembers Sarah, and they invested in themselves. By day, they flipped through their books of collected meishi, telephoning customers and coaxing them back to the club. Hostesses earned more if a customer requested them by name (a practice known as shimei), bought drinks in their company (a system known as 'drinkbacks'), or asked them on a dohan (to accompany a customer on an outing away from the club). With bonuses, a successful Roppongi hostess could earn a million Yen a month (around 9000 US dollars). 'They looked like they were putting all their energy into it,' notes Sarah.

Sarah also sang at an international hostess bar, a dark cavern with burgundy banquettes and low tables arranged around a large dance floor. There are regulations as to how dark a club can be. Clubs can be prosecuted if they dip the lighting levels too low. The darker the club, the greater the opportunity for customers to grope the hostesses. This cavern was very dark. Sarah worked her vocals through a middle-of-the-road repertoire: the Carpenters and the Beatles and the kind of 'cheesy' love songs that bring tears to the eyes of middle-aged Japanese men; while on the dance floor tall foreign women in stiletto heels swayed from side to side with section chiefs and under-managers pressed to their bosoms, or 'cheek-to-cheek time,' as it was known.

The foreign hostesses, ice-blondes from Eastern Europe, Russia and the USA, revealed more skin and deeper cleavages than the Japanese girls; and they didn't use their real names. A noticeboard in the changing room ranked girls by popularity, fomenting an atmosphere of high competitiveness and barely concealed animosity. The girls vied with each other for bonuses and those who failed to attract enough shimei or to achieve the minimum eight dohan a month fell to the bottom of the ranking and were fined or fired. Rivalry sometimes spilled over into fights with cries of, 'You stole my dohan! I needed that dohan!'

The international hostess bar teetered on the precipitous ledge of Japan's mizu shōbai (water trade, the business of night-time entertainment, traditionally termed 'the floating world') above a dark chasm of sexual exploitation and human trafficking. The international hostesses were illegal workers without visas or legal protection. Periodically, when the manager received a tip-off that police officers were patrolling the area, the club would close down for the night and the hostesses warned to disappear. Sarah was repelled by the seedier, more desperate side of bar hostessing. She soon fled back to the security of the little Ginza snack bar.

The international hostess bar teetered on the precipitous ledge of Japan's mizu shobai above a dark chasm of sexual exploitation and human trafficking

Indeed, the Ginza bar represented a home of sorts, much like the bar in the American television comedy show *Cheers*, 'where everybody knows your name.' A lot of the patrons had been drinking there for many years and Sarah reminisces, 'they would describe our place as "family".' Like a lot of snack bars in Japan, it was a members-only establishment with potential new members introduced by trusted regulars or brought in by a hostess and presented to the mama-san for approval. In the privacy of the bar, customers were free to behave with the abandon of wild little boys: to get drunk, to wear their ties round their heads, to leap about on tables; and to indulge in the make-believe that a group of young women really were overawed by their humdrum office jobs and flattered by their lascivious talk. Within this protected space, the true purpose of hostess bars became clear.

The Japanese economy is built on long-term business relationships that are cemented out of work hours in bars and clubs, places where alcohol serves to relax all parties and enable them to speak frankly. This is why public drunkenness, with unconscious salarymen passed out in the street and commuters stepping deftly around pools of vomit on station platforms, is largely tolerated in Japan. A conspicuous display of wealth is a key feature of many hostess clubs because most customers are not paying out of their own pockets but from corporate entertainment budgets, money allocated for entertaining clients and cultivating relationships with future business partners. At the Roppongi gentlemen's club, a hostess's birthday would be celebrated with champagne fountains and, Sarah recalls, 'the whole entrance to the building would be lined with gorgeous flower arrangements all bought by her various customers, all trying to show off how much money they had.' The Ginza snack bar was a much more homely affair but still the mama-san did not charge on the day; she sent out invoices at the end of the month, not to individuals but to companies.

Sarah met her Japanese husband in a salsa club. Before they married, she took him to the snack bar to receive the mama-san's approval. She continued to work at the bar twice a month, quitting reluctantly before their first child was born. She is still in contact with some of her customers, many of whom she counts 'almost as friends.' She sent them photographs of her son when he was born.

She worries what will happen to the snack bar when the mama-san retires. For a time, the mama-san employed her nieces in the hope that one of them might wish to succeed her. But what was once a full-time profession for women in a society in which they were deemed peripheral to the male-dominated workplace is now a part-time option, a way to supplement another income. Even the hostesses at the gentlemen's club had bigger dreams. 'They were saving up for something else that they wanted to do in the future,' admits Sarah. Most Japanese hostesses quit when they marry. The foreign hostesses leave when their visas expire (or when they are deported). Hostesses are transient figures in a floating world.

When Sarah began working at the little Ginza snack bar, the mama-san gave her some words of advice. She told her that the work was fun and that is was good to work hard but she should never view hostessing as a career. 'And that's the best way that you can get the most out of this job,' agrees Sarah. 'Don't get in too deep.' **H**

Salt EST. 1999

CELEBRATING TWENTY YEARS OF SALT

NORFOLK & NORWICH FESTIVAL
CELEBRATING 20 YEARS OF SALT
with Andrew Cowan, S.A. Harris, Andrew McDonnell and Simon Okotie
SATURDAY 25 MAY, 7.30PM
National Centre for Writing, Dragon Hall
https://nnfestival.org.uk/whats-on/celebrating-20-years-of-salt/

Great books, all the time

American boys are fast

but not
as fast as
ginger boys

by Michael Kineman

Towards the end of our first week of Year One, Mrs Davis told us to fetch our kit bags from the cloakroom and return to our chairs. We were then instructed to change from our uniform into our games kit. So we undressed, awkward and nervy: unsure what to expect from this new lesson that required us to strip down publicly. As we did, I started noticing a pattern. Underneath their button-up shirts, the other children wore a form-fitting white garment that covered their torso. I'd never seen this kind of shirt before. I gave a self-conscious glance down at my pale chest and protruding ribs, then looked about the room for a companion in my rising embarrassment. But everyone, boys and girls, were wearing these strange, sleeveless shirts. Many of them were already staring back at me, as I stood there semi-naked before a room full of people, as in some dream of social disaster I was yet too young to be haunted by.

'Why aren't you wearing a vest?' A boy at my table asked.

I turned back around.

'A what?'

'A vest,' he said. 'It's the shirt you wear under your proper shirt. Why don't you have one?'

I hung my head. I didn't know why. There was some laughter at my table, and another boy tried to help me.

'Americans mustn't wear vests,' he said.

By now the laughter was spreading to the surrounding tables. Clarity suddenly came to me: I needed to act quickly to avoid class-wide ridicule. I snatched my shirt and shorts from my kit bag and scrambled into them. Safely clothed, I sat down and buried my head in my arms until Mrs Davis told us to line up.

Things didn't turn out so bad as I imagined. After one or two more lessons I got used to being the only child whose chest was on display and the other kids mostly lost interest. Once I stopped worrying about changing in and out of my clothes, I found that I quite liked PE. We played games like Stuck in the Mud, Red Rover and Rounders. Over dinner I explained these games to my parents. It was sort of a competition to see who could be first to identify their 'real' names.

'Baseball!' My dad yelled. 'You're playing baseball! I thought Brits played cricket?'

I shrugged. 'Mrs Davis calls it Rounders.'

'Right, but you hit a ball with a big bat and run around the bases to home plate.'

'It's kind of a small bat actually, Dad. You only use one hand.'

'A one handed bat? How are you supposed to smack a home run when you're using a pie crust roller?'

Stuck in the Mud proved more difficult to explain. They were familiar with the basic concept, but not with the terminology. Being 'on' was called being 'it' and a 'tig' was a 'tag'. The game itself they called 'freeze tag'.

'What'd you call it again,' my dad asked. 'Glued to the dirt?'

'Stuck in the Mud.'

'Stuck in the Mud!' He laughed, his mouth wide and belly quaking. 'That's a pretty good name for it.'

But as summer approached, the games we played changed to those of a more serious sort: the egg and spoon race, the wheelbarrow race, the all-house relay and the mini-marathon. These were the events we'd compete in on Sports Day, a near-legendary occasion held during the last week of term when the weather was warm and the whole school went out to the playing field for games and no lessons. This utopian idyll hardly seemed possible to us Year Ones, yet Mrs Davis confirmed its truth. Best of all, I found I was naturally good at the races: I could run full speed clutching spoon and quivering egg, my hands were rapid as my feet when it came my turn to be the wheelbarrow, and the Red House elected me to run the final sprint of the relay. But by far the most important event was the mini-marathon. This one lap chase around the whole playing field determined who was the undisputed fastest in each year: a status that every boy hungered for.

The race started from behind the grey mobile classroom at the near end of the field and followed a narrow course around its edge, beneath the overhanging branches of trees and along the verge of tall, unkempt grass and tangled nettles at its shoulder. It felt good to let my legs go as fast as they could and watch others succumb to my pace.

By the home straight however, I found myself being outrun by another boy. I ground my teeth together, willing my legs to work harder – and I did gain on him, some. But he heard me coming, and his head swiveled to the side so that I could see his profile and his left eye, wild with determination. He too now surged forward and as my energy depleted his renewed. He was faster than me.

This one lap chase around the whole playing field determined who was the undisputed fastest in each year: a status that every boy hungered for

Aside from being the fastest boy in Year One, Rob Hale was known for three distinct characteristics. The first was that he ate Marmite sandwiches at lunch, which he would prize open and insert crisps into. The second was that he wore exclusively grey shirts, rather than the white that everyone else wore (a handbook-permitted alternative that went widely unrecognized). The third was his densely freckled complexion and near-luminous ginger hair. I considered all these characteristics carefully in trying to figure out the secret to his speed.

Although Rob was the only boy to break from the traditional ham, jam, or cheese sandwich (or the peanut butter and jelly that I preferred), after deliberation the other boys and I determined there was nothing incredible about Marmite – aside from its awful smell and flavor. A boy called Gregory was also known to eat the foul stuff, and he was near enough the slowest kid any of us had ever seen.

Nor were grey shirts known to do much: England's away kit was grey that year but the result was the same. The lone remaining factor was Rob's ginger hair. What else could it be? It was determined that American boys were fast, just not as fast as ginger boys.

Rob's mother met us at the school gate.
I'd been invited home for tea.

'Hello, Michael!' she said, as though we'd met before.

I returned her greeting, but directed my reply more towards the tarmac. She was a large, sturdy woman with sheets of frizzy ginger hair that fell to her waist. She scared me slightly, but then I was also shy – and meeting the family of my former rival.

Ever since our school field trip a few weeks back, Rob and I had become friends. I'd spied a discarded cigarette butt and dared him to smoke it. He plucked it from the pavement then paused to look me in the eye. His whole face contorted with a grin that seemed more of a snarl, then he jabbed the flattened stub between his lips and gave a deep drag. Eyes closed. Chest rising as it filled with forbidden worldliness. The exhale too was executed with the conviction of a stage performer: the cigarette hand drifted casually upward, as though rising to wave at someone in the distance, and a sigh issued from his cracked lips with the soft sensuality of a craving slaked. It was as though he'd been smoking all six years of his life.

We burst out laughing.

However, Mrs Davis heard us, and we soon found ourselves scolded in front of the whole class with – what I thought to be – an unusual amount of anger. I hadn't realized what we were doing was wrong, only a bit gross perhaps, but Mrs Davis was furious. A disgusting habit, she called it. We should be ashamed. Rob told her that I'd dared him. I shook my head in adamant rejection. Mrs Davis lowered her face until it was even with Rob's and asked him whether he'd be equally inclined to jump off a bridge if I had dared him to. Neither of us had encountered parallel reasoning before. It silenced us – would he? Either way we both had to hold one of her hands for the remainder of the trip – a calculated humiliation. I did feel a good degree of guilt, but despite that found it difficult to suppress the urge to howl with laughter whenever Rob and I locked eyes.

The Hale house was old. The carpet sagged under my feet and even when the lights were switched on they never seemed to banish the shadows lingering at the edges of the room. Although these things would have normally made me feel uneasy, they didn't, and that was probably because the whole place smelled golden brown, like living inside a cake hot from the oven. The source, I found out, was the bakery that the Hale family lived above and that Mr Hale owned. Rob's mum warned us to play quietly, because Mr Hale slept in the day and worked all night to bake everyone's bread.

This meant that when we watched TV, the sound

was so low I couldn't understand much. Running in the house was not allowed and neither was playing football in the garden. My favorite way of playing quietly turned out to be racing Rob's slot car set. On the back of the box were track layout suggestions, which we momentarily scanned before settling on the obvious (the figure of eight, as it yielded the most collisions). We fitted the plastic sections together, then picked our cars. Formula One cars were the fastest, Rob said, and he chose the blue and yellow Williams because that was Nigel Mansel's car and Nigel Mansel was English, like Rob. I was left with the white and red McLaren of Ayrton Senna.

'That car is fast too,' Rob said, sensing my disappointment. 'Senna was world champion.'

'He was?'

'Yeah. Three times.'

'Was he American?'

'No, there aren't any Americans in F1.'

'Why not?'

'They're not fast enough. F1 is only for the fastest drivers in the world.'

'Oh,' I said, feeling vaguely insulted. 'Well is he still world champion?'

'Who?'

'What's-his-name.'

'Oh, Senna.' Rob shook his head. 'No, not anymore. He got pushed into a wall at the San Marino Grand Prix and died.' I looked down at the car in my hands with a tiny replica of the dead man sitting inside. 'But that car is still really fast,' he insisted, setting his own car on the starting line and handing me my throttle. 'You might beat me.'

But neither on the slot track nor on the playing field was I ever faster than Rob Hale.

One afternoon my dad arrived at the school gates just in time to see the end of our PE lesson. He stood at the edge of the playground with his hands sunk into the pockets of his red letter jacket and observed our now well-established mini-marathon routine. From the start Rob sprinted out in front with me close behind. We ran until ragged and by the home straight Rob was beyond catching. Perhaps sensing my increased determination that afternoon, Rob turned and ran backwards before crossing the line. He grinned and waved at me and I hated him for it. My dad clapped as I crossed second. 'Alright, buddy!' he called. 'Good job!' But I avoided his gaze and went inside to change.

The next day my dad was waiting again, dressed in his red letter jacket but this time with a stopwatch hanging from his neck. He told me to go get my pumps and meet him on the field. As I sat in the short grass and changed out of my Velcro-strap shoes, he used the opportunity to give me some coaching.

'I watched you run yesterday and it seemed to me that you ran full pelt from the moment Mrs Davis said go. About halfway round you got tired because you'd used up all your energy,' he paused. 'Now I want you to try and work on running at about seventy-five percent for the start of the race and saving the rest for the final stretch. So when I say go, you start out jogging then about three quarters of the way round I'll yell 'Now!' and I want you to run as fast as you can all the way to the finish. You got that?'

I nodded, but I didn't really. Who ever heard of winning a race by not running your fastest? My dad's strategy made no sense, but I kept my reservations to myself and showed him an approximation of the starting line behind the grey mobile classroom. He told me to line up and I did, even though I couldn't focus. Every child and parent in the school was walking past on their way home and they were all curious.

I slowed to what felt like a comical pace, as though I was pretending to run rather than actually running

'Ready,' my dad called, loud enough for everyone to hear. 'Set. Go!'

But instead of dashing off, I didn't move.

'No, Dad,' I said, quietly. 'It's ready, steady, go.'

'Huh. That's really how they say it over here?'

I shrugged. 'That's how Mrs Davis says it.'

'Alright,' he said. 'Well if that's how they're going to say it on the day then that's how we'll practice it.'

We reset and this time he got the words right and I began running. However I forgot his coaching almost immediately: my instinct to run as fast as possible was too strong. Halfway around, my dad shouted for me to come back. He reminded me to not run all out until he gave the signal. When I returned to the starting line a group of older boys were waiting there too. They'd got the idea of what we were doing and wanted to race. I looked at my dad, desperate for him to send them away. They were older and I knew I couldn't beat them.

'You run your race,' he said. 'Don't worry about them.'

At first I again ran as fast as I could. I wanted to prove myself to the older boys.

'Slow down, Michael!' He called. 'Seventy-five percent!'

I slowed to what felt like a comical pace, as though I was pretending to run rather than actually running. The path along the edge of the field was bathed in deep, cool shadow and the air was speckled with gnats that hung about me at my reduced pace. I resisted the urge to run faster and as I rounded the final curve, bursting into the late afternoon light, my dad at last gave the signal. My palms tightened and my muscles strained and I gave that last third of bright ground all that my legs had to offer.

That night as I lay in bed, my dad told a story.

'Did you know back when I was in high school I used to run track too?' I hadn't known that, but neither did I doubt it. It seemed my dad had done and succeeded at near enough everything there was to do in life. 'Coach came and recruited me for the team after he saw me run in Phys Ed. I was thin and wiry – but quick – just like you are.'

'Really?'

'You bet, buddy! Now Highland was a little

rinky-dink school out in the country and the Anderson Indians had all the fastest athletes – boy would they beat us like a drum! During my senior year we had a meet scheduled up at Highland on our little dirt track that went around the outside of the football field – not a nice professional-style track like they had at Anderson. Coach came up to me that morning in the halls and told me he was going to put me up against the county champion on the final lap of four by four-hundred relay. Just try and stay on his tail, he told me. Boy was I motivated. I walked around all day with my chest puffed out like I was hot stuff – I was kind of a goofball head back in high school.'

I laughed at that funny pejorative, a favorite of my dad's. He continued. 'Well it rained most of the morning. One of those great big Indiana thunderstorms where the lightning illuminates the whole sky then you'd count – one one thousand, two one thousand – to see how far away it struck and when you felt the floor shake and the window panes rattle, then you'd know whether you were going to be alright or whether you needed to get down on your knees and pray!' He laughed at his own joke, then continued.

'Boy I miss a good thunderstorm! Anyway, it had been chucking it down all day and threatened to rain us out, but in the end it cleared and we went ahead with the meet. The relay was last and from what I remember we got off to a pretty good start – but then even that wasn't good enough against the Indians. By the time I got the baton, we were behind. Well me and that county champ took off around the track, and on the last curve there was this humongous puddle covering the inside lanes. Mr County Champ tried to avoid it by running along the edge of the water, but since I was behind and didn't have anything to lose, I just decided to motor right on through that puppy. Sent that brown storm water flying up over us both! Mr County Champ didn't know what had hit him. I went into that curve behind and, by the time we came out the other side, boy was I in the lead – smoked that guy by gunning it right through the middle of that thing!'

'What happened?' I said, breathless, like I'd just received some prophecy.

'Well he gave it everything on that straight. Tried to pass me on the outside, but I was not going to let him by. I'd made up my mind. I held him off by muscling him with my shoulder and that race was history,' he paused. 'The fastest guy doesn't always win, did you know that, Mike?' I shook my head. 'The race is not to the swift, that's how Solomon said it.'

'What's that mean?'

'For one thing it means that on paper that guy was way faster than me, but it didn't matter because he wasn't on the day. It also means that just because Rob Hale has beaten you every race so far, it doesn't mean he's going to next time. On Sports Day I think you're going to run like the wind, buddy.'

Dad and I continued with our after-school training routine for a couple weeks until one morning Mrs

Davis approached me before registration.

'What were you and your father doing out on the field last night?' she asked.

'We were practicing,' I said.

'Practicing for what?'

'The mini-marathon.'

Her lips became thin and her eyebrows rose, but not with surprise.

'Do we not already practice the mini-marathon frequently enough for you, Michael?'

Everyone on my table fell silent. I wasn't sure what the correct answer to this question was, but I sensed the importance of answering correctly.

'May I ask why you were practicing last night?' she said.

'So I can get faster. My dad is helping.'

'I see. Well, that is not the purpose of the mini-marathon and neither is it the spirit of Sports Day here at Fairoak First School. I must say I'm surprised at your father – especially being a vicar. I shall have a word with him tonight. You will not be practicing for the mini-marathon anymore except during PE lessons, just like everyone else.'

I cried every time I ever got told off in school. It always felt personal to me, as though the teacher was saying 'I do not like you, Michael.' Other children defied authority – denied they'd done anything or claimed the rules weren't fair – but I could never work out where they got such self-confidence from. Even if I didn't know exactly what I'd done wrong, I always assumed teachers knew something I did not.

I'd seen Mrs Davis scold many children before, but this was the first instance I could recall of a parent being reprimanded as well. This made it worse. I was devastated that my family were implicated in my moral rot. Although Mrs Davis held my dad responsible, I could not. He was American and his American-ness couldn't be helped. He didn't notice the frowns or the tuts of disapproval like I did. He just didn't get it, and this time neither had I.

I'd seen Mrs Davis scold many children before, but this was the first instance I could recall of a parent being reprimanded as well. This made it worse. I was devastated that my family were implicated in my moral rot

The remainder of the day dragged by as if it were a decade. I spoke to no one and declined to play with my friends at break or lunch. When the bell for home finally rang, I abandoned my dad and instead went to the cloakroom. I stood in front of my peg and busied myself with putting things in my bag then taking them out again until everyone had left. When at last I emerged onto the deserted playground, he was waiting with a smile. I hugged him and thought he was brave for such an unaffected response to what must have been a savage attack. On the way home he informed me that we would no longer be practicing after school. By his estimation it didn't matter much anyway: Sports Day was only a week away and my legs could use the rest.

'Those Brits sure tickle me,' he said. 'Sportsmanship she called it. Where I come from we call it hustle and it's considered a good thing!'

He gave a mischievous smile in my direction and I looked away. He still didn't get it.

Sports Day was a windless and cloudless summer's day among a long spell of such days that year. There was a track of white racing lanes sprayed onto the withered grass and a crowd of parents, two and three deep, surrounding it. Our head teacher, Mr Richardson, paced the field with a megaphone, announcing races and their winners. He also gave cautions about the heat of the sun.

'Use sun cream,' he said, 'and do wear your hats.'

I was singled out as a laudable example of proper hat-wearing form. I wore my stars and stripes baseball cap backwards, and Mr Richardson said I was very sensible for wanting to protect the back of my neck. Of course that was absolute nonsense – I was only copying older, cooler boys I'd seen wearing their hats similarly. My parents stood at the front of the crowd next to the finishing line. My mother held a camera and my father a camcorder. I waved at them and they waved back.

My first race was the egg and spoon and I won it comfortably. Next was the last leg of the house-relay, which I crossed in first place for the Red House. Then finally Mrs Davis lined us all up for the mini-marathon. I got a good position on the front row and felt my chest shudder with adrenaline.

'Ready – steady – go!'

A rush of feet and runners that thinned to two by the first bend. Along the shaded and endless back straight. Whoops from students and parents all the way down. My pace measured like we'd practiced, yet Rob Hale not far ahead. As we rounded the final curve I heard a loud voice boom over all the other voices and noise of the day.

'Now, buddy! NOW!'

I expended all that was left in me and was amazed to see the gap between Rob and I close. The whites of his eyes widened as he searched for me in his periphery. I drew level. Our shoulders scraped together and we jockeyed for position. This was the closest I'd ever come, but there was nothing left and I knew once again I would not beat him. But then, inexplicably, as we exited the final curve, Rob ran the wrong way. He soon realized his mistake, but it was too late. I surged ahead. My confidence and speed increasing with each stride towards the unobstructed finish. My dad's reddened face and outstretched arms directing me home. Mrs Davis smiling on the finishing line but her arms folded. My name drifting over the playing field as Mr Richardson announced it into the megaphone. I had won the mini-marathon.

That night before bed, my dad and I sat together in the lamplight, victorious conspirators. He was delighted, but somehow I felt hollow.

'I didn't beat him, Dad.'

'Sure you did, buddy. I watched you!'

'No, I mean I didn't really beat him. He ran the wrong way. I wasn't faster.'

My dad rested a large palm on my back.

'Races aren't just about who's fastest but who can hold their nerve. You could've run that race blindfolded, which is why you didn't get confused by all the people or strange lines on the field. Circumstances don't matter. You crossed that line first, buddy!'

He was always so sure of things. Optimism came easy and hung about him; everything else fell away as though repelled by some inner force. If he were in my place, he'd return to school and shrug off accusations that practice amounts to cheating. He'd believe he was the fastest in Year One, even if everyone else said otherwise. This was a lesson I could neither learn from observation nor

He'd believe he was the fastest in Year One, even if everyone else said otherwise. This was a lesson I could neither learn from observation nor absorb through his stories. His reasoning was that of another world

absorb through his stories. His reasoning was that of another world. I did not doubt its veracity on some other shore, only its relevancy to Mrs Davis' classroom. It was a distance between us: one that he could not see and I could not explain to him. I still depended on his interpretations and guidance – yet something had changed and this frightened me. Rather than respond, I buried my worries with a request for a story.

That night my dad did not source his inspiration from a bygone America. Instead, he narrated the day's events as he would one of his own tales: employing choice phrases like, 'gunned it', 'motored along' and 'smoked him'. I listened to his climactic account of the mini-marathon in rapturous disbelief, as though such a feat must have happened to some other boy in some other time. When he finished, I asked him to tell it one more time and he did. Then he pulled the duvet up over my shoulders, kissed my forehead and closed the door behind him.

'Dad,' I said.

The door reopened slightly. A narrow stripe of hall-light raced across the floor and his face reappeared through the gap.

'Yeah, buddy?'

'Can you leave it open a little?' ▉

Cullerfornia

by Helen James

I opened my eyes and looked across at the table by the bedroom window to see two books resting there. *From Black and White to Color* is a folio of photographs by William Eggleston, the other is a larger, unwieldy volume called *Cape Light* by Joel Meyerowitz; two American photographers who trade expertly in colour and light.

From Black and White to Color perches carelessly at the table end. A fraying red bookmark emerges from the letter E in the publisher's imprint at the foot of the spine. The bold capitalisation of S T E I D L sits square, classic and proud, each letter given enough space to breathe before the next arrives; a celebration of minimalist typographical design. The book is a perfect album size: yellow and cloth-bound it has the feel of a lost dust jacket, and looks like a box of KODAK photographic paper. The cover is embossed with a red bar that houses the words of the title and reveals them from the yellow beneath.

I know exactly which picture the bookmark hurries me to: sauce bottles on a table someplace in America – does it really matter where? I shuttle to the back of the book to discover I am in Louisiana in 1980. The picture sits inside the book like a postcard or a favourite snap pasted into an album. It's a very quiet observation; perfect for my photographic delectation. My eyes consume this image like a favourite poem, tirelessly returning.

Cape Light has recently been re-published for hungry consumers and is typical in its fashioning as a photo-book. I have another Meyerowitz book called *At The Water's Edge*; it's small, tiny even, and perfect for trips to the sea-edge in my jacket pocket, protected in a weary orange envelope that will never see a stamp. These are irresistible images. Both books are filled with pictures that harvest the gold to be found in photographers' eyes when looking is slow and observant; scanning every place to find visual excitement in minute adjustments to light, time and perspective. Waiting and watching for curious and attractive instances to happen.

My bedroom has a bay window that looks out at Cullercoats Bay and the North Sea beyond. From the bed I can usually see a crack of the day outside. Sometimes orange pours in or a grey steely light flattens and deadens everything. At other times I awaken to the foghorn from the lighthouse and wonder what colours are left outside.

When things are bathed in gold or a halo of orange and yellow I am hypnotised, yet my camera usually lets me down. I watch from my bed as shapes are sharpened or diffused by the intensity of the sun: a magical studio with an invisible director. I start each seaside day observing lighting displays unfold before the constant straight line of the horizon, always reassuringly still. On strange, misty days it melts away as sky and sea merge and everything seems flat and already two-dimensional; the editing has been done and the world looks surreal.

I feel guilty for looking at the world in this way. It seems indulgent to celebrate photographs that simply consider light, and are about nothing more than the collision of elements on some table or in front of some horizon. But light deadens the darkness that exists in every life. Even a chip of the sun glimpsed through the lilac tree in my old Norfolk garden was sufficient; just as a tiny glint of gold flowing over misty, early morning fields past the suited shoulders of Cambridge commuters is enough to soothe and distract.

I look out of the window and watch the sea gently wander back and to across the sand, inching like fingers hoping to tickle. White foam bubbles play silently under the line, messy and windblown. The cliff-top café over the road attracts people whatever the weather, its tables empty of sauce bottles. The building conquers the end of John Street, parking its triangle into an expanse of pavement that flanks the roundabout. Light can stream through its windows in three directions to create the perfect environment to sup and chat. Silver bistro tables catch the sun outside and are scattered over the pavement, just enough room to pass through lapping dogs and chattering mums. Grandparents clutch babies in matching nautical stripes, shades at the ready for a perfect seaside photo. When the closed sign is flipped on the café door the tables wait like an empty studio, while surfers sleep horizontally in vans outside, waiting for homemade coffee by the sea tomorrow.

I hurriedly pull my discarded jeans and jumper back on and hear the door slam behind me as I head towards the sea to listen and watch. I blew up the east coast from Anglia to Cullercoats, away from some dangerous cowboys that I met in the wilds of Cambridgeshire. Here is far enough to avoid the reach of a lasso that had tightened around me for the last few years. I head across the harbour beach and up the stone steps to the cliff top, until Longsands beach rolls away in front of me. Empty ships are parked perfectly along the horizon and a cluster of surfer-shapes dot the top of each wave. Set after set curls in and dissolves, rubbing away as many footprints as possible with each visit. I wanted to be near the sea that harboured happy memories along the littoral zone of Longsands. Everyone I know is here in the wind, whispering to me.

As I walk down to the sea I glance up at the cliff top and remember my sister walk away, tucked up and warm last Christmastime; she waved as she disappeared out of view. I hope she will be back soon. We had walked and talked about how odd it was to be adopted and to be page one in the family album. I was a few days old, she a few months, when the photographs started to bubble up and flow.

Each time I walk towards the lighthouse I lean over the harbour wall and gently hear my son Alex ask 'have you found what you are looking for?' with his cheeky humour and Liverpudlian tone. I turn around to look at his strong face underlined with a fisherman's beard but he has already gone. He is with me on every coastal walk. I remember him showing me the ways of the sea and the creatures that looked different unmagnified in his hand that he'd collected from the seawater of some rock pool; tiny hands clutching grasshoppers in fields and grown-up hands showing me a closed sea anemone on the causeway to St Mary's lighthouse. I couldn't find them without him, it wasn't important when he was away.

My other son Cal belongs here. His golden hair crafted by the wind and sea; Liverpool accent lost on his Geordie soul. He is always out there in the water; the subject of my searching eye.

Occasionally I catch sight of a surfer in Cullercoats Bay heading towards the rocks and wonder 'Is it Cal?' I watch the surfer climb on and off the board, mesmerised time and again by these sea people. I watch how they use the sea and respond to its moods. It calls and they show up clad in black suits and wade in. I will never know what it feels like to dangle my feet over a board with toes pointing at nothing but deepness. I don't have a desire to be in the sea, just to be near it.

Not all photographs need to be caught - they can be observed and allowed to disappear. Just like the surf that flows and dissolves without a rider on its

crest. When the surfers are out earning and the sea
is empty, it comes alive for my searching eyes.
I want to run and gather them from the jobs they hold
elsewhere but the best moments are disconnected
and unexpected. Lost is a magical country.

As I walk across Longsands I look for Cal's van
parked above the beach by the mighty Grand Hotel,
its red neon lettering booming loud across the bay.
I might see him in the sea if I am lucky. In the murky
waters I can only watch and scour the tiny figures
for something I recognise. I don't want to photograph
him in the water, just watch him rise, fall and walk

**He knows the sea in a different, more intimate way
and I listen to his watery tales. Tales of awesome
waves, inquisitive seals and sea-thrashed limbs**

the length of his board until he tips elegantly off the
end to rise once more. My memory is happy and
full; no photograph would serve it well enough.

He knows the sea in a different, more intimate
way and I listen to his watery tales. Tales of
awesome waves, inquisitive seals and sea-thrashed
limbs. Surf shanties; his stories not mine. I listen
to his perspective of the land from low in the
sea, far from the shore. When I look through the
photographs he has taken they are different to mine.
Less detached, sometimes harvested from the sea
itself, complete with a wobbly view and unsteady
horizon. I can sense the balance of the board on
the water as an uneven base. Gone are the details
that fascinate me; these photographs are unique
and sometimes devoid of colour. We both leap

away from trying to match the tones and motifs of a Californian summer with waving palm trees and rollerblading beauties under clear skies. The gentle play on words that prompted a local to coin the phrase Cullerfornia is draped in sweet Northern wit from the surf-loving culture of North East England. Pitch perfect. We all look for something different here. For me the soft visual repetition of Meyerowitz is worth listening to as his slow camera collected changes in light and shifts in perspective from a porch that looked out at the North Atlantic horizon. Our level straight line that underlines the end of the North Sea as it reaches the sky is a backdrop waiting for audiences and players. ∎

W. G. SEBALD

Far Away —
But From Where?

11 May–18 August 2019
Mezzanine Gallery

To mark what would have been the 75th birthday of W.G. Sebald, this
innovative, interdisciplinary exhibition combines rare and unseen archive
material. For the first time the wealth of UEA's archive collections and
the Sebald Estate will be used to explore Sebald's use of photography.
The exhibition will also showcase works by Tacita Dean, Tess Jaray
and Julie Mehretu that relate or respond to his writing.

Part of **Sebald Season** in association with Norfolk Museum Service
Image credit: W.G. Sebald, *Austerlitz Sequence*, Paris, December 1998
Photographic print. Courtesy of the W.G. Sebald Estate

SAINSBURY
CENTRE

University of East Anglia

SAINSBURY CENTRE

University of East Anglia

WHAT'S ON

The Body Observed: Magnum Photos
23 March–30 June 2019

John Christie
My Blue Heaven
10 May–1 September 2019

W.G. Sebald
Far Away–But From Where?
11 May–18 August 2019

Image credit: Andy Crouch

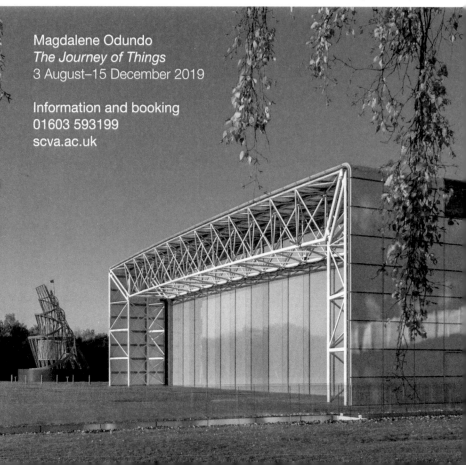

Magdalene Odundo
The Journey of Things
3 August–15 December 2019

Information and booking
01603 593199
scva.ac.uk

Second Time Around

by Justin Kern

Under the blue dawn of late March, the light off the Mississippi River reveals a humbling spread of mud on the border lands between Illinois and Iowa. I pull into East Dubuque's shitkicker downtown, in the shadow of a steel arch bridge that extends over the river and off-ramps into a police station, diner, strip club and third-shift bars with who-in-hell-cares names like 'R Place' and 'The Cave.'

It's my second time here in about three months, a reporter based two hours away in Waukesha, near Milwaukee. My connection is a found body that may be the missing son of a celebrated former Waukesha sheriff and current Wisconsin federal marshal. Months since that son went unguarded and sloshy into an East Dubuque December night, I'm in this same few-street town again precisely at that point in time between the identification of the marshal's son's body or just some body, between a person and this missing person.

East Dubuque started 150-plus years ago as Dunleith. On the other side of the Mississippi, Iowa's city of Dubuque never felt the need for geographic forenames, a sense of place built by college towers and church steeples poking above the Driftless Area topography. So, I guess, East Dubuque just gave in on the name thing. But it held its own through a state border town recognition of what's absent, like the anti-blue law stores on highways in New Hampshire, or the manic, vaguely patriotic firework warehouses that outline Indiana.

In East Dubuque, the bars open earlier and close later, barely close, really. For Dubuque, those bars make its neighbor a rugged little brother that beckons with distant similarity, over the bridge walkway or roadway, maybe even over the water, wet or frozen. For those living on the Illinois side, they're not that Dubuque, but they're somewhere.

My first time in East Dubuque, just after Christmas, I coincidentally met the federal marshal and his wife minutes after driving into town. They were walking out of the police station toward the diner, and stopped to talk with me. His flat face of flesh-on-iron was more honest with me than anyone deserved when enquiring about his son, who days earlier was last seen on this very street. First off, he wanted the public to know that he loved his son and he'd do anything to have him back. Then, procedurally, he explained how he ran these searches many times on his own as an officer of the law, each search taking people into the nearby pathways and the woods – always the woods – as well as into the backgrounds of anyone who fit the time, place or description. Beyond the process of a job, what this man held in his un-pierced expression was conviction, the hope of a father. The wife, not the son's mother, clung to her husband with care, like a sculptor to a piece newly shaped.

Talking with them at that moment, and from that time on, it was hard to shake that I was about the same age as their son. (For the story, he was always a son, but, he was by all definitions his own man: at twenty-four years old, with jobs and college and, by this juncture, the threat of death) Dishwater blond like him, and alike in how I drank too much and had been known to wander off, into bad hours when only anything can happen. As such, I left a few details on the son's partying history out of the initial stories – seemed no predicator of his fate – until later police reports made those tickets and trouble relevant. More: the father stared through my pupils as he hadn't with the other, weathered, balding reporters also circling his story.

As for the son, he had been to Dubuque to visit a friend. On the night in question, they partied their way into East Dubuque, the son leaving at a hotel his coat, wallet and phone. He was separated from the friend on being denied entry, or kicked out, of an 'exotic dancing club', and then walked on, a set of steps in each direction across the snow, including onto the iced-over Mississippi. A cop downtown saw him walking away from that club at 1.10 am on December 24th. What could be...

Cable TV news producers had started to call me for background in January, with hopes that this story hit on their heartland horror superfecta of young, white, on vacation and missing. It may be those things, I said to Nancy Grace's underling, without the same spurious conclusions people draw from apparition killers upriver in La Crosse. Plainly, to TV reporters, this son may have plunged through the ice atop the river, all on his own. Their interest soon dwindled.

The pair noticed a trash-draped tree stump floating in the middle of the river near a curve dubbed 'Deadmans Slough'

Forward, to the March morning a body is found in the warming, murky river. Over the phone, the federal marshal says he's 'anxious' about the discovery of a body. No speculation without identification. Been through this before. Never commented on how many people he had found alive, simply lost or taken.

Still in East Dubuque, at that version of the present, I scribble from the slim, early police report the name and phone number of the person who found this body. A local pilot says he had been flying his pontoon plane on touch-and-go manoeuvres, a practice whereby you take off and land, circle the airport and never really stop before doing the whole thing over. The wash-rinse-repeat instructions of flight, he explains.

Along for this exercise was the pilot's sixteen-year-old daughter. Up above, the pair noticed a trash-draped tree stump floating in the middle of the river near a curve dubbed 'Deadmans Slough'. Closer inspection led the daughter to call 9-1-1 with the suspicion that they had spotted a human in the water. Her hunch had precedent. Last summer the same father and daughter, flying in the same plane, eyed the body of a Dubuque man floating along the same section of river adjoining Deadmans Slough.

This all comes through over the phone, the pilot's voice plain, his daughter nowhere to be heard. Straightforward, on spotting in the river the new body in question, the pilot states: 'That's an area where, when there are drownings in Dubuque, that's where they end up.'

The view from on high. To round out my story, I need a few more voices on the ground to tell the impact of the body of a man they probably never knew in a town where that's not so weird. Who's around this groggy place at mid-morning, and not already at the bar or out fishing? A reporter listens to who's available to talk. This man-on-the-street randomness has imbued the opinions of drifters and shopkeepers with an inequitable clout in shaping the collective voice of small-town America.

I visit a library, auto body shop and boating supply floor. A pillowy lifer at a convenience store near the river promises worse in summer, if history serves.

'My grandmother used to live around here and said people go missing all of the time, but not so much anymore.' Rifle through the East Dubuque regulars, then back to the local police station, where there's an announcement. Today's body indeed belongs to the marshal's son. Death by drowning. Autopsy and coroner's inquest to come. I call the marshal, but his phone goes straight to voicemail for what turns out to be a week. I'm a fool for not asking earlier, before the body was named as one of his own, though the exact line of questioning continues to escape me.

By summer, a panel will tell the coroner they couldn't quite determine the reason the son's body was found drowned; and that explanation will be good enough for most people. Years afterwards, once the marshal is retired, his other child, an older son, would also die in sudden and publicly reported circumstances.

Back to that March, from the farthest map blot northwest in Illinois, I drive, bleary, back to southeast Wisconsin through the living daylight. Spin the word 'convicted' around in my head until it assumes all of its meanings at once, locked away, doubtless, diehard, to love. What could be, what could be. Stop, nap in my '98 Taurus, parked behind a hotel that could be in North Dubuque or South Beloit or Midwest Anywhere. Then, back on the road hurtling toward my desk to type type type and bring today's strife to life tomorrow in a story of the past. No agenda but time and enough truth to keep from having to explain in print how regular guys always seem to die for no good reason or why that teenage girl keeps going on flights with her dad when all they do is fly in circles and find stranger's bodies in the plodding waters below. **H**

Yocknapatafa

by Daniel Uncapher

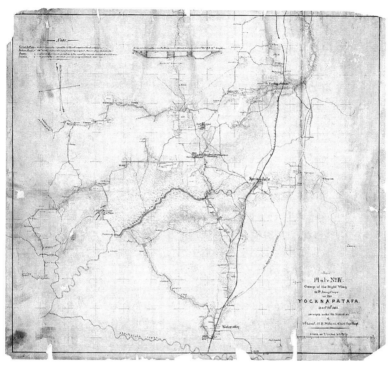

From the War Department: Plate No. IV. Camp of the Right Wing, 13th Army Corps, on the Yocknapatafa (Yocona River), Decbr. 21st 1862.

To stop the flood they dammed up the Yocona River and created Enid Lake, 1952. That was Leviathan work, Poseidon labor, and the Yocona River valley went dry.

In 1957 Freddie Bright pulled the biggest white crappie out of the lake that the world had ever seen, while on the opposite shore a local man abandoned a family of dogs at the boat landing (a beautiful campground, with all of the modern amenities), the so-called Water Valley adoption center.

The enduring undoing: war, credit, fever, waste, purgation. 1830: Treaty of Dancing Rabbit Creek, out-dealt the Choctaw; 1832, Treaty of Pontotoc Creek and the Chickasaw lose, too. Antebellum boom years (very brief time): time of the slave cabins and the Great Houses, the gold pulled from mountains miles long and buried eighteen inches beneath the backyard magnolia tree. Street fires, pony racers, Back Alley brawlers, the shroud falls over the hills as time inches onward in broad, intersecting arcs of creation, breakdown and stasis.

But Yocknapatafa isn't a historical narrative; it's a simultaneity of image and sound, of voices speaking in the present.

'Welcome to The Cedars. It was built by Confederate Captain S.B. Brown in 1862 using slave labor. The Yankees burned this town down twice but that didn't deter him. After the war he became a newspaper man and founded the paper that would become the storied North Mississippi Herald of today; he sold it during Reconstruction and served as the first superintendent of education for Yalobusha County. He may have been a signatory of Nathan Bedford Forrest's original terrorist cell, the Ku Klux Klan. The Cedars has a basement because it used to be a stable house on the Great Tennessee Stage Road, which would make it the oldest structure in town.'

Obvious lies and inconsistencies: too many oldest houses in town to count, three blocks uphill from the Great Tennessee Stage Road, probably not a signatory, just a sympathizer. Everything is ripe for denial and the people simply love it here, they have nothing but wonderful things to say about this place. The so-called artistic spirit. The murals – a Casey Jones commission, the old Coca-Cola ad, a drugstore realist cut-away in acrylic, a newspaper relic; we need more murals, they cry: paint the town! But murals cost money and need to be repainted now and then; and we only have one sign painter. He's overbooked as it is. And who will do the work?

The slave traders liked this valley for the cane and clear water. The first building in town was a slave cabin, and so was the second. That was back then. More recently a man with a teardrop tattoo forged too many checks and the police said, ma'am, there's nothing we can really do, but if you see him again on your property just shoot him. That's right, give 'em hell, brother. A man don't go his own way he's got nothing. Beat the milk-bitch up with my own fists, I did. What else could I do? Most people are good people, most people are in on the so-called social contract, but now and then you get someone in your life who just can't be reasoned with. What to do if you can't count on basic reason? A swirl of bad friends and bad hires, and the good one got himself stuck in a shoot-out at Sonic and was whisked back to Parchman, you know Parchman Farm, that Jim Crow cotton plantation where the Prison Writes Initiative takes up honest-to-goodness social progress, their progressive white faces smiling under the folds of all the regional papers.

As for me, I never eat at Sonic – their burgers are expensive, their fries are soggy; sometimes I enjoy a corndog, but I can't stand the sight of those fly-strips, heavy with flies.

Sonic's okay.

I love Sonic.

I eat Sonic every day.

Y'all want some Sonic?

Delivered fresh from the presses of the Clarion-Ledger in Jackson this morning, this week's edition of the storied Herald (dyed pink in support of the fight against breast cancer):

Ham and corn ads from the Piggly Wiggly, big shining coupon numbers; sent half the town in to get something to fix for the kids. Bagged red apples, discount lard, good brine, prime gizzards, the best tinned fish and oil-in-tubs that the Pig has to offer. The Dairy Manager works up such an appetite in the presence of pasteurized milk that he takes a

Bagged red apples, discount lard, good brine, prime gizzards, the best tinned fish and oil-in-tubs that the Pig has to offer

bath with his supper that night, the hot, bubbling oil percolating off his tongue, the black grit disappearing as if all at once from under his fingernails.

From Betty's front-page column: 'If folks driving on the streets and roads in and around Water Valley don't start being respectful of other motorists, we're going to have more accidents – and we already have enough. I had three very scary incidents last week.'

Community feedback: right as always! Loud music, no signals, young people – look who murdered the Wagners, for God's sake! Found the body half-buried in a ditch; pulled the perpetrator from the jailhouse and lynched him. That time! That time the freedman whistled at the wife of the railroad man so they hung him up, burned him, defaced him – what they did was right, declared General Pennypacker, but the burning was wrong. Pay-day riots, dead bodies shipped out on the night train, hide the evidence; uncoordinated schedules, crashed trains, overturned ferries, dead half-Indians by the wayside – probably drunk! (These are just reports.)

'WARNING! Automobile petting parties must cease. Automobiles containing men and women, boys and girls, and parking on side streets, by roads, dark roads, etc. both in the city and surrounding country, where petting parties and other obnoxious conduct are indulged in by the occupants, must cease. Parents are warned that their girls are in grave danger—and unless something is done to stop this thing, disgrace and shame will be the result. All "petting parties" are hereby warned that such practice must cease in this section—heed this warning before strenuous action is taken. We mean this thing must stop.'

—Yocona Klan No. 98, Knights of the Ku Klux Klan, Water Valley, Mississippi (North Mississippi Herald, September 11, 1925).

In 2001 two children moved down from New England and no one knew what to make of them. They entered High School in the 7th grade.

Coach Whose-Its took $40 from every student for Weekly Readers, bought a single so-called class copy and spent the rest of the dough at a riverboat casino in Tunica, open-sewer city of Sugar Ditch Alley. No one ever read that thing anyway.

A frizzle-haired do-gooder came down that same year to teach English and her 5th period stole the wallet out of her purse and robbed her blind on her own computer in the very middle of class. She moved back North and the students passed to 8th.

He stared at his feet, especially after the software measured his typing speed in regular excess of 120 wpm; he was a despicable typist. Teacher's pet, godless cur – what did he say? Vegema-what? He doesn't eat meat. What does he eat? Cornbread, beans – bacon in them beans – and greens? Like a whole hock of ham in those greens. Coach, haven't you heard? He doesn't believe in God. Well, she says, we'll change him.

Queer as a kite, he just sits there, staring – sunflower seed? No thanks: kernels, please, pre-shelled. Touch football. Straight as a rape whistle – fresh coke? Ice cold, straight from the cooler. Iced buns and cheese fries from the vending machine outside of science class, window units blown, coach sleeping, internet poker, fly strips, box fans, video porn. He noticed the unused televisions in the cabinet and asked after class if he could have one; the coach gave it to the kid, no reason at all, and he took it home to watch public broadcasting. They caught the coach sleeping with a student some time not long thereafter so he quit and got married to the little junior, settled down together, 9th-grade reading level soaking wet. (Then their son got sick at McDonalds and they had a lawsuit and became a millionaire and came back to teach and wore outrageous pants with colorful animal patches stitched into them, if you can believe that.)

Yes, there's some money nestled in these hills. Million-dollar ranch homes at the end of long gravel roads, pine-tar Republican aesthetics. Some classmates invited the new kids to a party and they rode out the long gravel roads together. Vodka-sleepover affair, mid-carpet bonfire, physical boundaries built and dismantled – anyway, who invited this kid? What's he doing, what's he listening to? And why does she spend so much time with him? She's so smart sometimes it's incredible, and hot, too. And he doesn't even look twice at her.

You don't need an opinion on everything, you know – what did you say about black people? She's no racist. Are you a racist?

Her grandmother said that he had a dark aura – do what? Don't listen to her, she's just a mean old witch – we're going to the lake, want to come? The Couches? That's the place. What're you listening to? Want to drive? No, don't go yet. Put up your phone. Come swim with me. Is that fish? Don't smell anything. Catfish?

They made a game of jumping off the sand cliffs. They called it cliff-jumping and there was no trick to it.

They wasted a lot of good money on bad movie rentals.

They call him a deviant. Everyone deviates. Faggot twins, everyone laughs; lanky worked at the brickyard got strong as an ox, earned a tuna sandwich and a bottle of vanilla milk each day. Fat cow got pregnant. Listened to Queen. Drug addictions – why else would they all shave their heads? They ran a train on her – white trash, good riddance – too drunk to stop them, I said stop – someone should put a stop to this, what can you do? Did you see the video? You don't need an opinion on everything, you know – what did you say about black people? She's no racist. Are you a racist? That's the problem with white people – what did you say about white people? Safe distance – stay in the distance, safe and afraid; visions of future mobility, driving far from this place on infinitely extending roads, fast dreams always moving – forward momentum, fungible time. Not tonight, though! Top search at 3 am: gay sex, big, ugly, illimitably extensible cocks. Nothing like it in the world – super mouthy, fleshy meat; pussy creamer risk-man, rub it around, rubber slows you down, rank and bacterial – asleep again, wet pants, fuzzy dreams of milky clouds; naked ladies spring up after the rain, pink and vibrant. Some things just don't get talked about. Oral masturbation testimony: well, we were just kids then, what happens as kids. Who were those devils, anyway? True Blue Devils: State champions, 1982. Or was it '86? What happens as kids stays with us forever. She grew her hair out and took a running start at it. Drunk as hell, they let her off again; Pontotoc Pontiac dealer cousin-in-law, big ad on the radio you know, Yalobusha plates. Opens his big book, crosses out names dues paid in full. When she was 6 a neighbor broke a crayon off inside her. Her father drank cranberry juice for breakfast. Her mother chain-smoked Pall Malls, pronounced pell-mells. Things changed, people relented; the ass-reamer picks up his falchion and goes hunting again—someone has to say something. Someone must speak out!

Emergency meeting convened at the Community Center by leadership elected and appointed:

We need developers! New construction – we have no investors!

It's the drinking laws! People want to drink!

You see what happens when we allow it – drunks in the street, we're not that kind of town!

Wal-Mart! A new trailer park! They're begging to build!

We're not that kind of town and never will be!

Manufacturing! We've lost the jobs!

Technology is the future! Coding camp – affirmative policies, angel funding!

Still time to get in at the ground level!

Artists, creative types, university people, young professionals!

No more artists, God no! We're simply not that kind of town!

Fix the schools! Build, build, build!

An artist colony! Affordable commune-style studio space re: unused manuf. facilities!

Gallery openings, wine tastings, by-firefly-light readings and art crawls!

Jugs Family Restaurant: Cummin' Soon!

Look how far a dollar goes: low rent! Historical district – Federal money!

Gig economy! Farm-to-table – too fresh!

Black church! Blues trail! Porous concrete! Crappie culture! Regional lit!

Some Indian saying 'Be the change', never heard of it.

Re: change, reports of lead in the water, no follow-up. Hottest summer on record. Scientific interest in the mold population. Resignations, no new hires, modular reforms, registration fees. Atomic breakdown – things cease making sense at their most basic level, but business presses on, collecting interest.

The atomic breakdown. Is it always this bad?
No, unseasonably hot this year.
Nothing stirs.
Newspaper articles with legible type: a derelict
town, resurrection, Crawdad, art community, other
familiar terms.

A so-called concrete movement: the old
woodsman starts sculpting concrete and concrete
sculpture takes the town by storm. The leaders of
the movement at the zenith of their cultural capital
petition the mayor to erect a concrete Colossus
over the north end of town, but the project is cut
off at the knees by the Christian coalition. Yards
transform seemingly overnight into pagan statuaries
and the neighbors erect two-storey wooden crosses
in retaliation; the pagans sculpt phalli in their rose
gardens and their neighbors stake white plastic
crosses like campaign signs by the sidewalks. On
the reverse side, in purple italics: He is risen.

Dry county, beer store at the county line.
Cradle of North Mississippi Methodism, meth
capital of North Mississippi. Drug runners in black
Mercedes speeding through Main Street 0300
hours, the deputy's Charger in hot pursuit – tinted
windows come down, shotgun appears, shots fired;
gun discarded, cruiser hits it and blows a tire,
disappears into pine country: good getaway.

A meth factory explodes and people mill on
the sidewalk in a daze; the neighbors can hardly
contain their excitement when they think about the
effect this will have on their property value.

Knock at the door 0245 hours: gas money...

sick grandmother. Dog freaks out! The man of the house doesn't even try to calm down his hound. Don't come knocking around here again, he says, smacking his shotgun against the doorway.

Meanwhile, at Rasputin's burger stand: y'all see that fellow riding that horse down Highway 7? 'Course. That's how he gets to work. You seen the way they live in Possum Holler?

150 years ago a rebel spy rode a shining black stallion through the valley and made for the wilderness; the Yankees caught him outside slavemaster James Knox Polk's plantation and executed him to great fanfare.

Are you not from around here or something?

$8/hr any day of the week. I'll take the job for $60/hr flat and hire two clowns off Calhoun, $16/hr under the table pocket the rest (can't explain that). Moon pies & a 40 for lunch. Calms your nerves, smushed flat, warm and ample suits your needs. Princess parasols on paving trucks. Better work than plucking chickens. The electrician lost it with the old broad and her fiancé beat his ass, then the dumb motherfuckers had an old-fashioned shoot-out down by Grinder's Switch. Went to jail for a spell, broke probation, folks beat down his front door and robbed him (took the state flag from the den window and everything).

Steak bone slide guitar: I just shot him; him dying was between him and the Lord.

Memphis-style pulled pork, please.

Hunger on a hot summer day: fried catfish, hash browns, crawdads, cornbread, okra on the plate, ranch dressing, pimiento cheese, mayonnaise on a pear, Jell-O salad.

Ate alright in Parchman, I can tell you that. Scared to death of prison; why would you be scared? People like you run the place. Went in with the Simon City Rurals – you mean Royals? What I said.

Get that gangbanger out of here!

I don't work for you anymore!

The one time I needed a penny the cashier stopped me and said, those are for people who need them

He'll fuck your father if you don't watch out! Cock in your father, cock in your –

Watch out!

Call the cops, dude.

But I need some work done on the roof. I need some windows scraped. I need a painter. Do you paint? I need a model. Male model; must do nudes. Art money, odd behavior. Terrible job – what did you expect? You hardly pay them after all, deserve to be robbed clean now and then.

I asked him what he thought about white people. White people have all the money, he said. Isn't that rich?

Sure, you can use the toilet. Is your washroom breeding Bolsheviks? I only use two-ply, no shit. My pipes are stuffed.

The one time I needed a penny the cashier stopped me and said, those are for people who need them.

Now the law don't come down here no more.

Magic square: liquor store, payday loans, bail bondsman, county jail. Magnolia Court in the shade of the courthouse. Dr Pullen, tooth-man, payroll puller – Methodist. Our Hearts Our Minds Our Doors. Opiate addiction – pure heroin, it's the least they can do. Cash-only. Waiting room Bible – don't open it! Last time she opened a Bible she became a Methodist, too.

Don't ever pay in advance. These are stupid people. They work for pennies. Boiled peanuts.

These are good people. Raised on the same television as anyone.

No—these are actual idiots. Not from around here, are you?

Tell your friend if I see him around here again I'm going to shoot him.

I understand; you'd have every right. (He always has to be right.)

Bango!

Pick up…

Pick up, please!

The sound echoes through the valley. Fireworks? Not this time of year.

Bango!

Here's the law now, coming fast. Act straight. You look beautiful tonight. After I killed my first deer my daddy cut its neck and painted my face with its warm blood. I took a big juicy bite out of the heart for the camera and daddy sent a picture to mama. I love my dad!

Did you hear? She took it in the ass in the service of the Lord. Theological loophole. Hot tub, splash around in hot filth – faithless actor, can't resist her. Sausage and cheese plate, everything on the table, red tomato ketchup in plastic bottles for the children.

Easy to work up a thirst in this weather. Boiled some bottom-feeders – spicy! Sweet smacking soaking-wet earth-writhers, blackened swine king snake-handlers; welcome back to the canebrake, tadpole place, Faulkner country. Peanut stand anticipation: heavy rain, a tall glass of water pulled fresh from the faucet (American Standard). Quench yourself! If you're thirsty then you're already too dehydrated. Don't be afraid – it's pure water, shiny stuff. Why are you so scared of the water? It's no Bell Witch. I said it's nothing to fear – you're no Emmett Till, are you? Roadkill Till, worked up a thirst and got his fill...

Bango! Bango!

That must be fireworks.

Anyway, if you're thirsty, go ahead and take a drink, but don't ever open a dialogue with these people; communication just makes it worse. The best thing to do in these instances is to buckle down and listen – sometimes they'll talk their way right into it.

Case:

In 1986 one of these Civil Rights heroes came to school for a pep rally and some friends – wasn't my idea – thought it would be funny to fly this big Confederate flag. We were all gonna stand up together and unfurl it as soon as she started talking. But when the rally kicked off I was the only one who actually stood up; boy did I get in some trouble.

Reporters came down from Oxford and everything. That was some goof.

What the hell are you on about? Quiet down and fix the porch!

Love this house. They used to build them smart, you know, in tune with the valley. Hallways run cross-ways like so to create a wind tunnel, you feel that breeze? You don't see deliberation like that anymore. People used to sit on the porch because it was the most comfortable part of the house. Community was easy then. Air conditioning made fools of us all. Even Faulkner was exposed by it. What was it he said to his daughter when she asked him to stop drinking on her birthday? No one remembers Shakespeare's kids. The first thing his family did after dumping his corpse was buy an air conditioner from Sears.

Shut your mean, hypocritical mouth and get back to that railing!

To understand the world you must first understand a place like Mississippi. Cretinous lie, of course. Mississippians are born-again liars

To understand the world you must first understand a place like Mississippi. Cretinous lie, of course. Mississippians are born-again liars.

If you quote that man one more time I'll beat your skull in with a brick like an Ole Miss riot.

He only got that big prize in the first place because of affirmative action—Swedish identitarian politics. Hollywood sell-out!

Shut up! Shut up! Shut up!

In the pre-dawn silence a Faulkner scholar from Toulouse, traveling with her French toiletries, hand towel and pillow, lays half-asleep in the old rope bed of her basement Airbnb at The Cedars…

I'd rather live with poor blacks than white trash. Trumpland, crucifixion country, he may be a n— but he's my n—. My south; the South is in my mouth (squeeze your thumb no gag reflex). After graduating cum laude he put down a claim on some land; if I want to fix this house I must begin with the foundation, he said. Mother tends the garden; old Bill moseys by waving hi. Lovely place to start a life. Beautyberries, blue dogbane, don't know what you'd call them; chickasaw plums, barely know them. Magnolia seeds like measled cantaloupe. An apple tree – heirloom number. Fig trees and their attendant wasps, Blastophaga psenes, burrowers, birthers, juicy decomposers. The façade is failing, the ivy seizes and rips. Corinthian columns, peeling paint; the window of restoration is passing. Two-year plans and five-year extensions. Kudzu out of control. Weather isn't looking good. Dubious reports of parasitoids in the water. That kid with Down syndrome was beat up again. Christian Today: 'Why I decided a child with Down syndrome wasn't right for my family'. His grandfather shot his father dead when they caught him molesting the 3-year-old again, now the grandfather is serving time. The judge was sympathetic but you can't abide vigilantes in this town. Whatever.

Snooze – she turns over, pulls a strand of hair from her lips, and dozes off for five more minutes…

Rain at one window, blinding sunshine at the next. Attitude adjustments, alignment of interests with house spiders. Everything is green, insistent green, too much oxygen, too much moisture in the air it can feel like a fishbowl. The machines in the basement are rusting out, irreversibly fast. Upkeep is impossible, simple entropy is more than enough to tip the scales out of favor. Tubs of cold vanilla ice cream move from one freezer to another and then into the stomachs of the hungry children. Show us your cock, Mardi Gras bra flasher, book collector, hayfield-style tractor-puller and lawnmower racer; her skin smells like bacon grease, he tastes like a salt-lick. What're you trying to say? Dinner on me, let's get out of here. Where should I come? Come wherever. Re: the navigable/unnavigable world. What kind of tree is that? I don't know. Why don't you know? Magnolia tree. No. Dogwood. How do you navigate the world if you don't even know your own oak tree?

Snooze – the clock falls off the dresser, lands safely in her coiled pants.

There was another rash of suicides that summer: Jimbo shot himself and sprayed blood all over his favorite dog, Bud, short for Bud Light. Bobby, who lived in the speed-addict folk hero Casey Jones' old house at the top of the hill, drank himself dead soon after. Then Sam died, and even the realtor had a go at it. What boring people they are. Boring consequences. Electric skies, inexplicable colors, heat lightning in broad broken ranks; the locals can't make heads or tails of it. They call it one

thing, then another – they talk in hushed voices,
they shake their fists at the telephone poles, they
hump in the dry heat of recycled night. Sheer
conscious labor: respiratory action, carbon cycling,
emotional duress, survivors of trial and error
and the mouth of the valley waiting for outsiders:
fetishizer supreme, other-man, the double-sex

They talk in hushed voices, they shake their fists at the telephone poles, they hump in the dry heat of recycled night

sword-swallower with 46 hands. Oh, you're from
Mississippi? Mississippi is no friend of mine. You don't
always survive your first overdose; the crappie don't
always bite. The weather doesn't always improve.

Snooze – the crepe myrtles beat softly against the
rippled glass and the cat stretches her claws across
the pillow...

In 2012 a team of reporters from the national
papers came to profile the renaissance. They
interviewed a group of beautiful white women
from out-of-town and told their full-of-hope tale to
America. 'I love this story,' said one American. 'It's
sweet and Spring-like and has real soul.'

Started awake – nights without sleep into days
without measure, the great white dream-time
steams on while our failures go wordlessly by –
unaccountably fast, they are gone. **H**

You couldn't make it up

The Real Story

DEVELOPING CREATIVE NONFICTION
AND THE ESSAY IN THE UK

The Real Story is a Manchester-based writer development project and online journal devoted to promoting the form of creative nonfiction writing in the UK. Funded by Arts Council England, we provide workshops, mentoring and a publishing platform for both established and emerging creative nonfiction talent. We're always looking for personal essays and pitches, so head to therealstory.org/submit and send us something wonderful and true.

Supported using public funding by

**ARTS COUNCIL
ENGLAND**

Hogiau Pen Garret

by Peter Goulding

Becky, Lee and I set out from Ty Powdwr, which is now a climbing club hut. The building used to be a gunpowder store for the Dinorwic quarries, it's just next to a much smaller structure called Ty Ffiws. Ty Powdwr's walls are two feet thick, made of stacked layers of slate. Originally, the roof would have been wood, with no metal used in its construction – not one single nail. It's sheltered by the hill behind it, but not from the wind or the weather. If the gunpowder had ever exploded by accident, the blast would have gone straight up through the roof, and travelled harmlessly across the empty valley – no iron nails to turn into bullets – although the few little cottages you can see would have had their windows blown out.

It's a stroll across to the quarries. The day is sunny and fetching out to be warm, not ideal climbing conditions. The rubber on your climbing shoes sticks less – its formulated to be at its stickiest at 5 degrees – and your hands sweat more, so we are heading over to the East Braich, a horseshoe ridge that curls around the huge quarry-working called Australia. This will be in shade all day.

My back is really bad. I had to lift a load of oak the week before, for not enough money either; building work is wrecking my body. Then, sitting still for the six-hour drive west from Norwich has thoroughly inflamed it. My thighs feel tingly and odd, and muscles in the top half of my back have been cramping as I hold my posture awkwardly, trying to take the weight off my poor burst discs. Thankfully, Lee and Becky are carrying the rope and other gear. The climbing I've done this week is helping stretch everything out, but I'm still not right.

As we walk, Becky and I chat about the stuff everyone talks about: work, family, study. She grew up near me in the north-east of England and did an animation degree at Sunderland. I've never met a climber yet who doesn't like films, but Becky explains in detail how to make an animation of a punch in the face really work, enough to make people flinch.

Becky is very unlike Lee: she's short, he's tall; she's dark-haired and light skinned where he is blond and tanned from working outdoors. She is chatty and outgoing to his quiet presence. Becky climbs hard – especially for her height and reach. She cares about it a lot, which is crucial for Lee. She is as psyched as Lee is; the rest is just detail. They look to me like they fit together.

We walk up, through the gate near Bus Stop Quarry, then follow the quarry road along the shady birch woods. Old drystone buildings are lost amongst sedges and reeds from pools where the water runs off the hill. Across the valley, up towards the pass, the plume of smoke from the steam train climbs Snowdon with another load of tourists. Further on is an old, long cutting shed covered in a rough cement render, its roof long gone.

—

Slate has a distinct set of physical characteristics. Millions of years ago in deep geological time, layers of clay mud or volcanic ash, carried by the tides of a tropical sea, were dumped out of the water as it lost the energy needed to transport it. The mud sat there, until it was buried by the movements of tectonic plates. Then it was baked at extreme temperature, extreme pressure, for millions of years, in the Earth's kiln. It became tough, and durable, but easily cleaved into flat leaves of stone. These specific characteristics made slate very useful as a building material, when people finally thought to use it. Large chunks could be split into thin tough sheets, and then nibbled into shape to form many different things: writing-slates for children in Victorian schools, the beds for billiard tables, gravestones, whetstones for knives, but, most importantly: roofing slate. These tiles could be laid into a roof that might last 100 years.

In 1962, British Pathé Pictures shot a short informational film about the Dinorwic Slate quarry. It is about two-and-a-half minutes long, and easy to find on the internet. The quarrymen work away, setting charges, driving small trains, hitting things with hammers, while orchestral music plays, and a voice in the newsreader's Received Pronunciation of fifty years ago describes how 'fyescinating' it all is. The voice-over starts with 'Few can resist the sight of men digging a hole, or indeed the hole itself,' and frankly, it's downhill from there.

The script's closing remarks are unintentionally perfect. Despite the modern locomotives and explosives, we are told that 'time has stood still'. Slate was quarried here much the same way one hundred years ago, and there is no doubt that in one hundred years' time it will be quarried in much the same way.

In 1969, less than eight years later, the hammer fell. The Dinorwic quarry was closed by its owners, who blamed a cancelled French order. Communities that had housed and bred the men who worked the pits were, at a single stroke, gutted.

Over another gate, now we are in the part of quarries where 'Public Access is Strictly Forbidden'. Up towards what climbers call Australia: the quarrymen called it Garret. It is a huge crater, as if a volcano has blown off one side of the mountain, except it was gunpowder that did the blasting: ninety tons of it per year over dozens of years.

The path up to Australia runs between the buildings visible on that old Pathé Film, now smashed to rubble. A few stumpy walls made of brick still stand, lined with ceramic tiles. This must have been a shower block. Coal mines, by law, had shower-heads at the pit-head for the miners. It must have been the same for the quarries.

We head up wide steps in the slope between Dali's Hole and the Incline, where great lumps of slate used to be winched down. Up the slope runs a strange concrete trough, capped with paving stones. This holds heavy duty electrical cables running up to the reservoir at the top of Elidir, which powers the sluices, gates and valves for the hydroelectric plant buried deep in the moun-tain's guts.

At the col halfway up the side of Australia, most climbers head to the levels on the western side, where there are low-grade sport climbs. It's often in the sun until late afternoon and is where I started climbing. Now, I want to push my grade and climb more challenging routes. We need the shade so we head to the right. The East Braich is hundreds of metres high. A flight of steps runs up its crest.

'What's these stairs called, Pete? A Welsh name, hasn't it?' asks Lee, which is a compliment in itself: he knows the guidebook by heart.

'Nah. The Stairs of Cirith Ungol: from *Lord of the Rings*. In the book it's the back way into Mordor.' Which is spot on, because there is a quarry pit called Mordor, the hardest part of the quarry to find, and this would be a roundabout way to get to it.

The quarrymen walked these steps every day if they had work up here, but they called them Llwybr Llynog, which means 'Fox Path'. The steps are wide and flat, and made of waste slate. Each roof tile wasted four-fifths of what was quarried from the ground, but the waste was well used. At any size, slate could be split into dead flat slabs and lumps, so it was easy to make plank-like sections that balanced on flat-sided blocks, locked together by their own weight, no mortar needed.

The steps are worn from hundreds of long-gone feet. The quarrymen wore wooden clogs, which polished the slate to a smooth shine, rather than scratching tick-marks like hobnails would have done. The steps are strewn with little chips and lumps of slate that have fallen or been carried by the water, so you have to keep an eye on where you tread. I've done enough on mountains with endless, boring snowy slopes, to know that the trick is to keep going, steadily.

It's hot, and sunny, and my back sweats clammy beneath my rucksack. The three of us plod up as the path curves round, no longer talking. I haven't counted the steps; maybe they are just a couple of hundred, maybe five hundred.

At the top, the ground opens out onto a wide, flat plain, shaded by a wall of rock. Where the steps end is a cluster of huts. The biggest and best preserved is the Caban hut. The cast iron stove is still there, never stolen – it would weigh a ton, and there's all these steps to get it down. Until a few years ago, the last quarrymen's overalls and boots hung from the pegs where they'd been left, until some fucking fool torched them.

There is still whitewashed plaster on the walls, with graffitied names carved in since the quarries closed. TREV and DARREN make their regular appearance, but I don't notice any of the normal toilet wall cocks. Amongst all the recent graffiti is a small panel that says 'Hogiau Pen Garret', which means 'the boys of Pen Garret'. There is a list of names: Jack Jones, Daffydd Esther, Arthur Owen, Robert Hughes, Wil Rees and Will Rhys, many more.

The caban was a quarryman's institution: the hut where the men gathered to eat. On the rockface men worked in small teams of three or four, but mealtimes were social, reinforcing the bonds of trust that were so important when your life depended on the man working next to you, rigging your ropes and setting the charges.

The caban was much more than just a canteen. Just as the pub or church were focal institutions in the villages surrounding the quarries, inside the pit the caban was the heart; a community centre controlled not by the owners but the workers themselves, where grievances were settled and whip-rounds, donations for the injured or bereaved, collected. The men sung and held poetry and prose competitions, debated politics and trade unionism.

It sounds unbelievable. The canteens I skived in on building sites never held a poetry competition. Playing cards for money, competitive swearing, sadistic practical jokes and unending racism, football and misogyny: that was the soundtrack to our break times. In those canteens you'd only ever find the *Sun, Star* and *Sport*. Detailed on football, most of the lads read them from the back to the front, where the articles turned into a load of bitter shite; murders by illegal immigrants, single mums claiming £27,000 of benefits per year. A colour picture of a 19-year old from Minehead with her tits out. Poetry competitions? No.

The quarrymen in the nineteenth century read Welsh-language newspapers: some aimed specifically at the quarrymen, maybe High Tory, more usually nonconformist and Radical. Heavy on local news, but with international affairs and politics, and usually a Poets' corner and short stories. There is no mystery really. Just the human impulse to be more than your job. If your job gave you status, some slight surplus of money, some free time in the summer evenings, then coal-miners and factory hands found things to do, societies to found, sports to play, rabbits to breed and pigeons to race. Inside the caban quarrymen could pursue these interests during the working day and outside the control of the owners, contributing to Welsh-language culture on the quarry's time.

The quarrymen spoke only Welsh whereas the managers' language was English; very few were bilingual. Typically, managers also lacked experience of quarrying; their backgrounds were in running brickworks or factories, where production depended on highly controllable factors such as shifts and the rate of work of machines. Fulfilling orders meant managing time and the workers. Quarries could not be controlled in this way.

This division in expertise between managers and the quarrymen, reinforced by their language barrier, led to the core belief that only the Welsh could read the slate.

—

Becky, Lee and I set up near *G'Day Arete*.
Becky walks around taking a few photographs.
There is a huge abandoned rusted steel bucket
that could fit a small picnic of people into, and she
frames the entire basin of Australia with it. There is
also a thick steel rope, running diagonally down the
cliff, with the rusted dolly that hauled slate up and
down still fixed in place. Lee and I hang onto it,
and do pull-ups; it doesn't budge an inch.

To warm up, I get on *Hogiau Pen Garret*,
named in tribute to that piece of graffiti in the
caban. It should be straightforward and it's well
within my grade, but there's a tricky move three
clips up, which I drop, and I'm left swinging in
space, Lee holding the rope below.

'Good effort, good fall, Pete!' shouts Becky. She
isn't mocking. Lee and Becky have got the same
attitude as me: it's good to fall. If you don't fall you
aren't trying hard-enough climbs, and by taking fall
after fall, the fear retreats and you can ignore the
consequences. I get back on and finish the climb.

A little later, I get onto *G'Day Arete*, which I really
want to get. It's graded at 6c, so it's possible for me
to do this, but not without effort. It's a great looking climb too, right up a clean edge like the corner
of a house. The slate is textured and grainy, and the
holds are widely spaced. There are little ridges that
require you to lay your whole weight on them to
work, and you have to weave around both sides of
the corner to find a way to go up. Tricky, and hard
to adjust your mind to.

Becky is belaying me. She is a good climber, really game, bold and skilled, but she is even better as a belayer: totally attentive, and confident enough to pay out enough slack for the rope to take the shock out of a fall, absorbing it into the inherent elasticity of the rope.

Two clips up, I get into a strenuous position, all my weight pulling side-ways on a hold, strength fading, and my feet not quite high enough to reach the next hold, a square ledge. Last chance, I try and throw my hand up, using the spring of my body to gain the extra centimetre I need. It works, but my feet cut loose, no longer supporting my weight, so sure enough I fall.

Becky already has the rope locked on her belay plate: my fall doesn't surprise her. I weigh more than she does, so I pull Becky right off her feet and up into the air, but she knows this is coming and jumps into the rock face, springing feet out, cushioning the blow with her legs.

'Thanks for the catch, Becky!' We balance out, both laughing. Her feet are just off the ground and I'm hanging about six feet above: I reach down with my hand and we high-five. Lee is grinning, he's taken photos of it all.

After this fall, I've had enough. It's not working for me today; I'm not climbing well and I'm tired. Lee and Becky head off down some sketchy ladders, bolted to the rock-face to find *The Road to Botany Bay.* I will meet them back at the hut. I am going for a moody walk around the top levels of the quarries, where few people go.

—

Winning the slate out of the ground was dangerous and highly skilled work. Shotholes were bored up to seven yards deep, with pneumatic drills. These drills were heavy and rattly, the quarrymen held them braced against their thighs and forced the drill bits into the rock. The vibration damaged the capillaries in the quarrymen's hands, eventually leading to White Finger, an industrial disease affecting the circulation and finger dexterity.

With the shothole drilled, explosives – sometimes a small paper-covered gelignite charge, more usually gunpowder – would be dropped into the hole, a cord of fuse threaded in and then sealed with clay. On the hour, every hour, a siren sounded and, wherever they were, the men lit their fuses, all across the various workings. The fizzing flame ran along the cord and up into the rock, while the quarrymen walked, rapidly, to the slate blast shelters nearby. A thump and a puff of smoke, amongst the dozens that echoed out across the quarry. The explosives had to be very carefully worked out: too much would just blast the huge blocks of slate into splinters, which was not the point. The idea was for the explosive to force open existing cracks, or run new cracks along the bedding planes.

The quarryman would climb down to the face from above, sliding on ropes, using his feet to brake the speed of descent. Their ropes were perhaps two or three inches thick, made of natural fibre like sisal, jute and hemp. When they had climbed to where they wanted to work, they wrapped turns around their waist or thigh to hold them there.

With six-foot-long iron pinch bars, they would prize the huge blocks free from the face to crash on the level below. In a way, these men on their ropes were the earliest climbers, although they didn't name their climbs. No point. Whatever they climbed down would be blasted off tomorrow, or the week after. They stopped working a face when it no longer became practical to, or when a hidden flaw – a ripple or dolerite seam – meant the slate would be no good for splitting.

———

I walk up through the old structures. Here, high on East Braich, most things have survived pretty well, the original build solid and skilful. Towers still hold steel rope skylines, dangling carts full of slate, frozen in the act of winching them up and down. Railway tracks – there were dozens of narrow gauge locomotives stealing in and out of the quarries – and inclines, sloped tracks, with big winding wheels, are still here, made of wood and cast iron. Nearly all this equipment was made on site, down at the bottom of the quarry, next to the lake. Joiners put wood together. Patternmakers made templates for cogs and pulley blocks, which Moulders cast in molten iron or steel. All this went up the hill, installed and assembled by millwrights and engineers. The technology tended towards the simple and the massive.

Finding my way about is an adventure in itself. This is not a waste of a day. I love all this, rambling and scrambling, seeing strange things, and unexpected views. Two levels up, I see a building, long – more than a hundred metres – and low, with its roof tiles missing but steel frames still in place. I enjoy the challenge of finding a way up to it, following an incline that offers an incredibly wide set of stairs with tiny treads.

I have found a splitting shed. Inside, there are dozens of circular saws. The toothed blades are still here, and the steel frames, and the big sheet metal cutting beds that the slate slabs laid on, moving smoothly on runners, to cut a dead-straight edge to the block. Everything is rusted orange. Holes have blown through the sheet metal with corrosion, and cast casings have cracked, perhaps when the roof fell in, perhaps smashed by someone bored with a lump of stone.

These sheds were where the Splitters worked. The Splitters were perhaps the most skilled craftsmen of all. Given a two-inch-thick piece of slate sawn into a rectangle, they would be expected to split out at least sixteen roof-slates, and nine to an inch was peak performance. Each roof-slate would be about the thickness of a pound coin. The splitter tapped in a long, wide chisel, running the split around the edge of the block, until with a last decisive strike, the complete tile would fall away. The feat was so skilled that slate splitting was one of the main competitive events of the Eisteddfod, as important as the poetry and singing competitions. Reading the slate was an emblem of Welsh culture and it's no accident that the development of the quarries coincided with a resurgence in the popularity of traditional Welsh language culture.

This splitting process converted slate from stone into saleable commodity and splitters worked long hours, day after day, perched on a stool. The defining industrial injury for a splitter was a bad case of piles, but the death rate and age was no lower than that of the quarrymen working with explosives on the pit edge. Clouds of slate-dust filled the air of the sheds and its particles were more reactive than coal-dust, which caused the infamous 'Black Lung' amongst coal-miners. When a grain of slate lodged in the lungs, the body formed a microscopic scar around it. This would have happened thousands upon millions of times in a Splitter's working life, with the inevitable progression first into breathlessness, then lung disease and death.

Some of the old Splitters still give demonstrations of their skill at the National Slate Museum in the old quarry buildings at the level of the lake. I saw it once, a room full of tourists and teenagers on a school trip. At the end of the demonstration, applause. One of the boys carried it on much too long clap … clap … clap, the sarcasm obvious. I could have fucking strangled him. He wouldn't have lasted a day up there.

At the bottom of the incline, I swing my leg over the gate, which clangs on its hinges. That's it, I am back in the part of the quarries you are allowed to be in.

The road sweeps out from here back to the gate at Bus Stop Quarry. It's a lovely easy walk, a bit of up-

and-down, but nothing grim. Everything fenced and safe, and big wire cages contain the rubble at points where the scree of slate waste threatens the path.

People may as well be wearing uniforms of their tribe. There are bird-watchers looking for choughs and peregrine falcons – they always dress in black and olive green, carry tripods and walk slowly because they're old. Runners stretch past in lycra, with funny arm pockets for their iPhones seamed into Hi-Vis running tops: they're usually old too. On an evening, you might see a load of teenagers walking together to a party they are having somewhere among the old quarry buildings. The girls dress smart and sexy in jeggings and strappy tops and the boys look casual and cool; a few years ago every third one had a pork-pie hat on.

Climbers look like climbers. Scruffy fuckers as a rule, synthetic fibre trousers that can dry in seconds but are cut to be ugly and utilitarian. Bright jumpers and jackets in bold colours, bobble hats and beanies. There is a whole set of brands you can spot, and a sliding scale of authenticity. The North Face means petty drug dealer, at the level of doing a deliberately obvious deal in a supermarket carpark; Mountain Equipment is what teachers might wear on playground duty, right the way to Organic, Patagonia and Arc'Teryx at the top. If you were really cool, you wouldn't bother with any of this, would you? But we must wear the colours of our tribe.

I've got my rucksack on. My helmet I've clipped to the shoulder strap, I like to rest my elbow in it as I walk, so – yeah. No prizes for guessing I'm a climber.

I walk along the road, through the Watford Gap, headed for another padlocked gate, and a family is walking towards me. Middle-aged Mum and Dad, lad about twenty and daughter late teens, all of them smartly dressed; trainers, Adidas, jeans and sweaters.

I smile and say 'hello' – I always do, and not just because I feel happy. Everyone said hello in the villages where I spent my teens.

They all return my greeting, and The Dad says "Ave you been climbing then?' Nice North Wales accent, I'd listen to it all day.

'I have, aye. Too nice a day not too, eh?'

We all agree it is.

'Yeah,' I say 'the slate suits me; I love it here in the quarries.'

The Mum looks at me. 'We like walking here. But a bit sad for us, because our Granddads all worked here, before it closed.'

'I know,' I say 'I grew up in the coalfields. Not here, up North.' It's a gesture of understanding, the demise of the pits isn't the same as the closure of the quarries, but something passes between us anyway.

A few minutes later I hop over the five-bar gate and down the hill, and back into the part of the quarries where access is forbidden. I should have asked them what they thought of us climbing there. ▉

Sabbatical Report

by Scott Coykendall

I spent most of my Fall sabbatical at a farmhouse in central Illinois, not far from the old US Highway 36, which runs straight as a mapmaker's rule from Eastern Ohio to Rocky Mountain National Park in Colorado. It's a major interstate in some stretches, but here, in the flat eastern counties it is a two-lane road. There are three hills (rises, really, to slip over or under a creek or railroad) and two curves between here and Indiana, 40 miles away. From my parents' porch, in the late Fall when the corn was done, we could watch an 18-wheeler come and go for five miles. Also delivery vans, pickups and farm trucks – but this is East Central Nowhere, so mostly the road was empty. Sometimes a turkey vulture or a crow would light on it. Sometimes the ambulance from Tuscola would rush by to pick up an old person from the Newman Nursing Home and take them, sirens screaming, 40 miles north to Urbana. Sometimes it glided past silently on its return.

We were waiting for my mom's death. She had stopped chemotherapy in the spring, but not until it had poisoned her blood and weakened her to the point that any exertion would exhaust her for days. She was supposed to die, according to Dr Rowland's prognosis, in the spring or early summer. But she didn't.

My mom was dying, but my dad – with his bad heart and his diabetes and his reflux – seemed to be racing her to the grave. He took terrific care of her. He kept detailed notes of every pill she took, every change in her condition. But when she did fall, as she began to in the spring, he could not lift her. On several occasions, he had to call his brother to come help in the middle of the night. Once, she was wedged between the bed and the wall so tightly they had to call an ambulance. I hadn't planned to spend most of my sabbatical there, and they didn't exactly ask. But they needed me, so I did.

One day in September, I climbed down from the porch and took the wheelbarrow and a bucket and sat under the apple trees sorting the rotten fruit from the salvageable ones. Mom watched from the porch wearing three sweaters and a pair of huge, old-lady sunglasses. She smoked a cigarette, then she got to her feet and came down the stairs to help. I was long past telling her what she was strong enough to do so I emptied my bucket and gave it to her to sit on and we scooted along beneath the trees tossing the soft brown apples into the wheelbarrow, piling those that were still solid enough to make into pies or applesauce into a small mound.

'So much wasted this year,' she said. 'Next year, I'll have to be better about picking up these apples. There's a case of applesauce spoilt in that wheelbarrow.'

I don't know what she believed. Sometimes she acknowledged that she was dying – mostly because I insisted on asking about her wishes. But more often she seemed to willfully pretend it was not happening. Pretending for me, or for her... I don't know. She was brave enough, submitting to all of the cold and chemical horrors of modern medicine with something like stoicism, but I think she preferred death to sneak up on her from behind while she pretended not to hear it.

She was brave enough... but I think she preferred death to sneak up on her from behind while she pretended not to hear it

Earlier that year, in the summer, we had visited her mother. Grandma was also sick with many of the ailments that people in their nineties must bear: diabetes, congestive heart failure, high blood pressure and so on. Recently, her toes had swollen up like apples and could not be touched without lighting the worst agony in her. I helped Mom into Grandma's trailer and watched while she, whose own hands often shook now, tenderly examined Grandma's feet. I knew from long conversations with Carol, Mom's hospice nurse, that the body is a quarrelsome republic whose end is signaled when the outer provinces begin to rebel. Mom questioned Grandma and Aunt Becky about the doctors' latest visits, about the bewildering list of medications she was starting and ending. And then, her energy suddenly spent, she asked me to help her to the couch. She was asleep in seconds.

I got her up thirty minutes later and convinced her that I needed to drive her home. It was almost four and I wanted her to sleep a little before dinner. For once, she didn't argue, didn't take offense that I was disempowering her. Near Philo, a small oasis on the left side of the featureless road with a bank and a Casey's and a restaurant that serves fried fish dinners on Fridays, Mom gripped her side. Her face went ashen.

'I have bad pain,' she cried. I touched the brakes.

'How bad, Mom?' I had picked up the routine from Dad. If she answered five to seven, I would give her 10mg of morphine. If she said eight to ten, I would give her 20. There was traffic coming so I could not turn left into the gas station parking lot or onto one of the shady side streets.

'Oh God, it's a nine,' she groaned. 'No, it's a ten.'

I couldn't stop in the road, so I took the first right turn and stopped beneath the shade of some spreading oaks. I reached into her purse and got out the box with her morphine and syringe. Dad had put a drop of red food coloring in it so that we could see the level more easily when we measured it into the syringe – always in haste. I pulled the plunger until the tube filled with 20 mg of pale pink liquid. Mom opened her mouth wide, like a bird in a nest, and I squirted the morphine under her tongue. She closed her eyes and pressed herself into her seat while I put the syringe and the bottle back in the box, and the box inside her purse. Then I reached for her hand and she gripped it tightly. We sat in the car while it idled and listened to the traffic cruise through Philo on its way home.

After a few minutes, she relaxed and opened her eyes.

'How bad is it now, Mom?'

She answered a five or six and looked around. We were parked in the narrow horseshoe lane of the Philo cemetery.

'Don't get any ideas,' she said. 'Get me outta here.'

I spent most of the fall in Illinois and came home to Plymouth for two weeks here and there, and then a few days here and there, to work with colleagues on the software we were developing. We ran a pilot study with nine faculty members and their classes in the fall. In my parents' house, with their spotty internet coverage, I was able to answer emails and resolve technical issues about the application. When I was back in Plymouth for a few days in December, we met with the participants of the pilot study and understood that there was still much work to do if the application was to meet our goals. We were, as always, torn between giving our attention to the application, and writing up research for publication.

I also planned my courses for Italy. Eighteen
months previously I had been approved to take a
group of students to Sorrento, Italy, for the semester
now approaching. I set up my parents' ancient
card table in my bedroom on the second floor of
the farmhouse. It looked out over the cornfield,
and then the empty field. I played Pimsleur

> **I pulled the plunger until the tube filled with 20 mg
> of pale pink liquid. Mom opened her mouth wide, like a
> bird in a nest and I squirted morphine under her tongue**

Italian Lesson CDs on my laptop and practiced
my conversation. I worked up the syllabi for the
courses that I planned to teach in Sorrento in the
spring and corresponded often with the faculty at
Sant'Anna. But I needed to be near Mom as much
as I could in case she had pain or she fell, so I
often took my iPad downstairs and read pieces of
travel writing while she napped. Often, I would be
sitting in the living room reading articles about the
Amazon rainforest, or South Sudan, or Venice and
Mom would ask what I was reading.

'Articles about Italy?'

'No, not exactly,' and I would explain that they
were articles for Italy, for one of the classes I was
going to teach. She would smile faintly and fold her
hands on her lap.

'I'm so glad you are going over there. You'll
never forget something like that.'

On one occasion, I put down the iPad and went
to sit with her. I wasn't sure how I could possibly
go to Italy with my Mom dying at home. It wasn't

that I wanted her to die before I left, but I couldn't imagine being on the other side of the planet when she went. I tried to say that without saying that. One day, while I held her in my right arm and lay my face on top of her head, she took my hand and patted it.

'I promise, son, I'm going to stay alive until you get back.'

It was a terrible thing to say. The night before, she had groaned and writhed in pain as the tumors gnawed at her. Dad and I gave her dose after dose after dose of morphine and Haldol and Ativan, morphine and Ativan, morphine, morphine…until it

The idea that she would endure that horror, the slow grind as her own body devoured itself, while I sat in the sun in Italy was a shot of pain even worse than the thought of her dying without me

closed the door on the world. I never knew if she was locked in sleep with the pain, or if it too was locked out. The idea that she would endure that horror, the slow grind as her own body devoured itself, while I sat in the sun in Italy was a shot of pain even worse than the thought of her dying without me. I thanked her, falsely, and sobbed as I did so.

Grandma moved to the hospital and then to a nursing home. I took Mom to visit her one day even though the Gilman Home was over an hour away. Mom asked that we stop in Walmart on the way. I pushed her around the store in the wheelchair and piled things on her lap. Cookies, bags of popcorn, a hairbrush. Mom was desperate to bring her mother some small comfort. Impulsively, I grabbed a bunch of flowers and piled it on, too. The nursing home was so much more elegant and bright than Newman Nursing Home, where my other, even-older grandmother lived. Lots of windows and skylights, craft rooms and social areas, an aviary scattered full of finches like confetti. I wheeled Mom down to Grandma's room where Mom and Aunt Linda fussed around her bed and Grandma complained that she didn't need to be here, she just wanted to go home. Mom was soon swaying in her chair and I had to beg her to let me take her home.

At Thanksgiving, Dad and I took her to my cousins' house. Aunt Linda or Aunt Beck had brought Grandma from the home and we wheeled Mom next to her. Grandma, looking terrible herself, was alarmed at how much worse Mom was. Mom slumped in her chair and soon asked to lie down. All the bedrooms were upstairs and Mom was too weak to get there, so they inflated a big air mattress in a small room off the den and we helped her onto it. At dinner, I pulled two of the tables apart and placed a folding table, the legs still up, across them so that we could wheel Mom up to one side and Grandma to the other. They both pushed their food around their plates and made a lot of noise about how good it was, but they might have had three bites between them. We left early and Mom slept in the front seat the whole ride home.

I flew home after Thanksgiving and in the five days that I was back in Plymouth, Grandma went into the hospital. My brother picked me up at the airport in Chicago and we stopped at Carle Hospital on the way to the farm. It was late when we arrived. Grandma was alone in the room and pneumonia rattled and knocked in her chest and she panted as she talked.

It was late when we arrived. Grandma was alone in the room and pneumonia rattled and knocked in her chest and she panted as she talked

'Oh there was a big crowd in here today,' she said. 'You couldn't walk through sideways.'

She asked us to look after Mom. She insisted we look after Mom. She said 'I love you' to each of us. Mom had been there all day and the next morning wanted to go back. But there was just no way – she needed help to get from the bed into her wheelchair – and she wept when we told her that she couldn't go. Grandma died in the afternoon; my brother and I sitting on either side of our mother as she cried that she should have been with her.

As the 'writer' in the family, I delivered the eulogy. Mom sat in the front row in her wheelchair and my dad leaned over to hold her hand in her lap. When I sat down, other grandchildren came up and spoke beautifully of her and one of her nephews gave a sort of sermon. Then Mom's minister – a reformed biker with gray hair to his shoulder blades and full sleeves of tattoos – gave his own sermon. In the car on the way to the cemetery, Mom slept and, when we arrived, had to be told where we were and what we were doing. Dad, my brother, my sister and I struggled together to push Mom's wheelchair over the uneven, frozen ground.

After Christmas, I stayed until New Year's Eve, then I had to return home. I had been at my parents' for 26 days straight and there was so much to do to prepare for a semester in Italy. That last week, cheered by the presence of my daughters, Mom actually looked better: no longer using the wheelchair, staying up for longer stretches. She had already lived months longer than the most optimistic predictions; maybe she would make it until I returned from Europe.

I returned to Illinois two weeks later, one week before I left for Italy. The night before I got on the plane to Chicago, we were laughing on FaceTime about which restaurant I would take them to. Mom said she had finally come around on Mexican food and she wasn't going to just split a plate of something Dad liked. It was the usual ordeal to get there: drive to Concord to catch the bus to Logan, fly to Chicago, take the el-train to the Loop, walk four blocks to Union Station, take an Amtrak for two hours to Champaign where Dad would pick me up and drive me the last hour to the farm. Mom had stayed up to see me. She was sitting on the couch with her legs crossed reading the paper when I came in, her reading glasses at the end of her nose. She stood up and hugged me and insisted, before I went up to bed, that I eat a rice-krispie treat she had made. She didn't have to twist my arm, exactly.

The next morning, I was first up and Dad came out 30 minutes later cleaning his glasses with his handkerchief. He made Mom's coffee and set out all her pills as well as his own while I looked out the window at the gray ribbon of Highway 36. It was sunny. Mom came out on her own and we all ate breakfast while I filled them in on the problems I'd had with the Italian consulate denying me a long-stay visa. They were worried that I would end up in some Italian jail but I told them that teachers had been overstaying their visas for this program for years. My departure (odds were that it would be my final departure, as far as Mom was concerned) loomed over us all morning, but goodbyes would be tonight after dinner out on the town. For today, we were just trying to be together and normal.

But Mom asked for morphine at 11am: pain in her left side under the ribs. She needed more at noon. And 12.30. And 2. By 4 pm, we had given her more morphine than she had ever had in one day and the pain was twisting inside her like an augur. She cried and writhed in her sheets. Dad stood and held her hand while I shifted from foot to foot wondering if I could get anything that would help. By 6, she had had over 160 mg of morphine and was still trying not to scream. There would be no Mexican restaurant. Dad and I took turns eating leftovers while the other sat with her.

Around 7pm, I went in and lay down on Dad's bed and held her hand. She couldn't open her eyes much, but she could talk. I asked her what she thought was next. By that, I meant, are you afraid to die? She told me she planned to plant flowers in the spring. She wanted my sister, June, and my wife, Tabitha, to come and help her. Simple flowers like petunias and rose moss. She told me how proud she was of her irises and the ornamental grasses and how much she loved to arrange the rocks she had brought home over the years from New Hampshire. And then she said she was sleepy and I got up and left her alone.

My departure loomed over us all morning, but goodbyes would be tonight after dinner out on the town. For today, we were just trying to be together and normal.

An hour later, the pain attacked again. She started to scream. And cry. Dad gave her 40 mg more, not even bothering with the 20 increments. After 240 mg, she lay still. I got him to sit on the couch instead of his recliner so I could hold him while his body heaved with fear and grief.

Uncle Wayne was coming to get me at 5am so that I could catch the 6.10 train from Champaign. I tried to wake Mom to say goodbye but she could not be roused. Not even a groan.

She did not recover. I talked to her on FaceTime the night before I flew to Italy. My brother and sister were with them but she was swaying in her chair at the kitchen table and not making much sense. The day I landed in Italy, I called home and she was too weak to say more than a few words. A couple of days later, Dad had to ask the hospice to take her to the Newman Nursing Home, down the hall from his own mother, so he could have a much-needed respite. Once there, it became apparent she wouldn't leave. June called and said Mom couldn't speak, but they thought she could hear and would

I like to talk to her. I was sitting on the couch in my apartment in Sorrento when I told her I loved her and that she had raised us well. That we would see each other through this. That it was OK to go. June, or maybe Mark, asked me to describe Sorrento to her, so I stood at the window and drifted into a rambling description of the beautiful umbrella pine outside my place, the orange and lemon trees and olive orchards, the sea and the mandolin music until I had used up all the words.

She died an hour later, on January 30, exactly one week after I left the US for Italy. I slept deeper and longer that night than I had since I left home. Grief doesn't wake you in the night as fear and anxiety will. When the sun was up, I ate my breakfast standing at the window and went down into the streets of Sorrento. I kept my eyes down as I hurried across the Corso Italia towards the ancient marina to sit by the sea. On the deserted Vico Strettola San Vincenzo, the olive trees dropped the last fruit into the nets spread atop the wall. I'm told uncured olives are bitter and unpleasant. Hundreds had escaped the nets and they rolled down the gutter ahead of me. Mom would have clicked her tongue and shaken her head at the waste. I kicked olives down the street, put my face in my hand and leaned against the wall, wishing stupidly for a bucket. ∎

You thought you knew the whole story...

Come and celebrate with us at Untitled writers' events - a new platform for underrepresented writers to share their work in front of an audience. There are no limitations to what might be shared and we know there'll be something for everyone.

To find out more about Untitled, let us know if you want to share in the future and to find news about our next event, visit **untitledwriting.co.uk**

 writinguntitled untitled_writing

The Women at the Station

by Saloni Prasad

I am stuck in the narrow passageway of a general bogie reserved for ladies and my whole life is flashing before my eyes. There is a woman standing at the front shouting at me. My eardrums are bursting. I am stuck. She is stuck. Behind me is a long queue – as long as the tiny bogie permits – and behind this angry young woman are the wild bison, cramming their way into the coach that's already filled to the brim. 'Let us out first!' Another woman screams and pushes me from behind. And I, both leading and blocking the line of angry goddesses who want to get off and get on the train at the same time, don't budge. My bag is in an unbreakable embrace with the suitcase of the woman who is swearing at me. And I am quietly listening to her.

'Move woman! Move!'

But I can't.

There is something called unreserved coaches in Indian Railways. Travelling in these coaches will cost you the least. There's a catch, though. The seats are to be taken on a first come, first serve basis. That means there is no guarantee that you will have a place to sit. General bogies tend to be very crowded but, if you are a woman, you might try getting into another coach called ladies bogie. These work on a first come, first serve basis as well, but since the number of female travellers is comparatively less, you have a greater chance of finding a seat.

I am in this mess because I didn't buy myself a ticket for a reserved coach. Since I had to travel I decided to try the ladies bogie, which to my misfortune, was crowded as well.

I boarded the train anyway.

The coach is tiny. They always are. I was neck to neck, sweat to sweat, with my fellow passengers. But things were fine. Things were tolerable. The problem started with a woman sitting on the floor (because obviously we don't have enough seats). She had blocked my way to the exit, which was fine, because there was still time until my destination. I assumed that she would get up when the train came to a halt at the station.

I forget how uncommon common sense is. Ultimately when we told her to stand and make way, she took an eternity to do it. It was as if she were in slow motion. By the time she cleared enough space for us to move ahead, the passengers on the other side had already started to rush in. The result of her stupidity? Absolute chaos.

'Move! Woman! Move!'

I am probably going to get old here. The hostile crowd surrounding me isn't exactly a good environment to spend the rest of my life, but what can I do? The woman at the front is still swearing. My suitcase is still stuck. I am stuck. And I am beginning to see death.

Maybe it isn't death. It is God. The woman stops shouting at me and decides to cooperate instead. She lifts her bag and I am able to step ahead and drift my bag forward. This is progress but there's still a long way to freedom. There are too many people. My suitcase is creating havoc. As I push myself and my bag forwards, I accidentally hurt a child who is standing in the way. Her mouth forms a gigantic O, her cheeks turn red, her eyes start shedding tears. Her mother glares at me.

I want to apologise. I didn't mean to slam my bag into her foot but seriously – *will you just shut up?*

I am never going to get off this train. These women, this noise, this wailing child have turned this place into a hell and I haven't sinned enough to deserve it. I have already started formulating alternative plans. I start thinking what the next stop of this train will be and how I will get back from there.

'Move! Woman! Move!'

Woman can't move. CAN'T YOU SEE! Woman is stuck between all these people and shouting doesn't help.

All of a sudden, amidst this great struggle for freedom, comes a helping hand. But the helping hand isn't polite either. Helping hand is angry.

Helping hand is shouting at me too.

'Itna late kyun aa rahe ho? So rahe the kya?' Were you sleeping all this while? I glare back at my messiah, the red-shirted coolie who is lifting my bag. He doesn't shut up. 'What a mess! What were you waiting for?'

'Would you stop shouting?' I yell. My voice breaks like the light splitting through a prism. I regret it at once. But it works – the coolie falls silent.

When I finally get off the train, I feel like I have been reborn. The coolie places my bag on the platform and disappears. Good, forget money, I wasn't even going to thank him.

But he helped you…

Shut up.

I avoid thinking about the near-fatal swarm of the women. I avoid thinking about the wailing child. I avoid thinking about the cuss words I have been showered with. I notice that my breathing is erratic and I am a bit dizzy. I sit down on a nearby bench, take a few deep breaths. I am alive. I am safe. I am safe! Finally I thank the coolie in my head. I resolve that I will never travel like this in the future.

A few days later, I find myself sitting in the unreserved ladies coach again.

—

There was a half-naked woman sitting on the platform. She sat amidst her luggage, combing her hair with her fingers as if nothing was unusual.

She was skinny. She had a wheatish complexion. Her hair was long and wet. She wore nothing but a petticoat. I looked at the people passing by. They too acted like it was normal. Most of them didn't even notice that she was topless. I looked away, embarrassed. I turned again to ensure I wasn't hallucinating. I saw her back, bare and exposed, a couple of vertebrae poking from within. I saw a man staring at her as well. So she was real.

How was this even possible? Wasn't this supposed to be culturally inappropriate? Am I in the same country where women have been catcalled for wearing jeans? Wasn't she risking her safety? Wasn't she 'provoking' anyone? I wondered if she was too poor to give a fuck. I wondered how no one else had stopped to wonder.

It doesn't make sense. I am a woman too. Why is this bothering me? I told myself I was staring because I was curious, not because I was a pervert. I was staring because this was unusual. I was staring because...

I walked ahead.

On my way to the exit, I came across some people who were sleeping on the platform. Among them was another woman. Her hair was brown, filthy and matted. It was tied in a bun. Still, most of her hair fell on her face. Her infant son slept beside her. Both of them seemed deep into their slumber. The woman's blouse had shifted exposing her breasts. I looked away in embarrassment. I looked to see if anyone else had noticed.

What is it today?

It's just flesh really. I have it too. I was bothered but the women didn't seem to care. I was bothered but the men didn't seem to care either. I was bothered because I'd been thinking the culture was still regressive, and now suddenly it seemed that it wasn't. It had accelerated into progression. And I was left behind.

I stepped out of the station. It was hot. Taxis and auto rickshaws were lined up nearby. A woman asked me for money. I ignored her. She asked again.

'Don't have change. Please go,' I said, not meeting her eyes.

'Madam? Auto? Where do you want to go?' Several men approached me.

Finally I replied to one of them, 'Vesu, how much?'

'One fifty rupees.'

The driver went to get his rickshaw from the parking area. I waited for him to return. I thought about the women I had seen inside the station. I wore a pair of shorts and a T-shirt. My hair was tied in a bun. I was sweaty and exhausted. And I was being stared at. A U-turn, sudden deceleration and society screeched to a halt exactly where I had been left behind. I couldn't understand how.

Maybe people outside the station are just more bored than they are inside.

—

Your eyes have a little green in them. Actually, no. Your eyes have a lot of green in them. How, given the fact that we live in the land of black and brown shades of iris, is that even possible?

When I first caught your glimpse at the railway station that day, I didn't want to move. As I looked at you, I realised that half of me was stunned by the sheer beauty of your eyes and the other half drowned in jealousy. I wanted to stay there and catch a better view of your face. But I couldn't have done that without making you uncomfortable. So I walked away.

As I looked at you, I realized that half of me was stunned by the sheer beauty of your eyes and the other half drowned in jealousy

Did you notice what impact your mere glimpse had on me? How could you? You were busy talking to your friend. And who was I anyway? Another face in the crowd. Ordinary black eyes, ordinary black hair, nothing interesting.

Would you have remembered me if I had told you how beautiful your eyes were? Would you have remembered me if I'd told you that they put a genius up there just to create your eyes. A bit of sap green in the palette, then he mixes a little yellow in it. Not too much – he is careful not to make it too bright. He paints it throughout the circumference of your eyeball. He lets it fade inwards into the brownish grey background of your hazel eyes. The green slowly diffuses into the grey. He uses the thinnest strokes. He uses the best paint brushes. The grey has a bit of brown in it, he blends it well.

In the middle, there's your pupil; jet black. Even if I try a million times I can't paint it the perfect way despite the fact that the image of your eyes is pinned inside my head. That's how beautiful, enigmatic, attractive, unusual, amazing they are.

Exaggeration.

That's what the voice in my head says.

You caught her glimpse. A glimpse that lasted just a few seconds! Maybe her eyes weren't green at all. Maybe it was just the angle. Thought of that?

What are you saying? The angle of light turned brown into green?

No, what I am saying is that she may have been wearing contact lenses the whole time.

———

'Chal bey Bhosdike Madarchod!' swears the bald old man.

Though I shouldn't be, I am pleased at how the drama is unfolding right in front of me. The old man is dressed in the colour of peace – white taqiyah, white kurta pyjama, white pair of slippers. He is shouting at another man, half his age, who stands beside a food stall ignoring him. I am sitting comfortably on my duffel bag, enjoying my coffee and the scene.

'Jaana Bhenchod!' the old man shouts.

He lifts his walking stick and spits on the ground. He is still ignored.

People are looking at him. He is too angry to care. He walks away. He returns.

'Bhosdike, teri maa chod dunga main!'

The young man at the food stall walks to him and shouts back, 'Gaali bolna band kar!' Stop swearing, old fool!

The old man swears even more loudly. Other men intervene and tell him to stop. Still he does not.

'Jaa kahin aur!'

A man pushes him away. Surveying the crowd that has gathered, the old man swears some more and finally walks off. The crowd disperses.

I have finished my coffee. My train is yet to come. I shouldn't but I miss the old man. I look around for some other entertainment. I catch a woman, clad in a green saree, sitting on the floor. She is staring at me. I stare back. She doesn't look away. Finally I do.

1-0

I scroll through the newsfeed. It's too hot to find anything interesting on the internet. I look at the random people passing by. A young man dashes towards the stairs that will take him to other platforms. Probably, he is late for his train.

'Been there', I mumble.

A girl runs towards the edge of the platform. Her furious mother catches her and drags her back. The girl still laughs. I laugh too.

I catch the woman in the green saree looking at me again. I stare. This time, she glances away.

1-1

A train comes and goes. It was a malgaadi – a luggage train. It had forty-two bogies. I look at the digital clock hanging from the roof. My train is ten minutes late. I wipe the sweat off my chin. I look at the hanging fans and realise how futile they are. The electrical wires are neatly tied in a couple of bundles, running in parallel through the roof, dividing it into four parts.

I turn and look at the woman. She is looking at me. I wonder what she finds so fascinating. I wonder if I am actually that good to look at. But nothing is communicated between us. She looks away.

1-2

A vendor passes by, pushing a small ice cream cart. 'Vadilal ice cream!' he advertises. I don't like Vadilal. 'Chai, chai, chai!' Another vendor comes and goes, holding a big aluminium teapot in one hand and plastic cups in the other. No thank you, I just had coffee. Fellow passengers are busy with their phones. Some are texting, some are watching a video, some are listening to music. My train is twenty minutes late.

An announcement is made:

'Yaatrigan kripya dhyan de, gaadi kramaank
– do nau nau che shunya, Surat Intercity Express,
kuch hi samay me platform no.1 pe aane vaali hai.'

The announcement is repeated in English:

'May I have your attention please - Train no.
Two-Nine-Nine-Six-Zero, Surat Intercity Express,
is expected to arrive at platform No.1 soon.'

A few minutes later, I hear the whistle of the
approaching train. It has arrived. Before I get up,
I look at the woman in the green saree. As always,
she is already looking at me. We stare at each other.
Nothing is communicated. I look away.

2-2

Such a weird woman, I wonder.
Which one? someone in my head replies. ▉

A trillion dollars.

The amount stolen each year from the world's poorest countries – and a number it would take you 31,709 years to count to.

'Eye-opening and essential'
New Statesman

'Pacy, clever and entertaining'
Guardian

'Every politician and moneyman on the planet should read it, but they won't because it's actually about them.'
John le Carré

Flashpoint
by Josef Steiff

There's a kind of bomb that leaves buildings intact, destroying only their frail human contents. A bomb so precise that you could be right next door and remain unscathed.

This is the fourth explosion, the one to finish what was started months ago. Your skin is still bruised, stained a greenish brown just now fading to yellow, the only shrapnel this kind of bomb leaves.

You've heard your life will flash before your eyes. You've always thought it might look something like this:

You're 5 years old, your bare feet sticking to the cool vinyl of the kitchen chair that has been left here in the bathroom just for you. You've dragged it over to the sink, climbing up so that you can reach the faucets all by yourself. You're about to go to school for the first time, wearing the brand new haircut your father gave you last night: a flat top. You watch your reflection brushing your teeth. You lift one foot and then the other, turning your head from side to side, imagining what the other kids will see when they meet you. Back and forth, back and forth. And that's when you see them: your ears. You lean closer to the mirror, no longer shoving the toothbrush back and forth into your mouth. Do other kids have ears? You wonder if you've ever seen other people with ears. In your panic you can't remember. What if you are the only one? Leaving the toothbrush stuck in your open mouth, you cover your ears with your hands. You want to cry.

You're 14, kicking your feet hard, swinging your arms over your head and then down, with each stroke pushing your entire chest out of the water, opening your mouth wide, a raspy grunt accompanying the rush of air you suck into your lungs before hitting the water again. Your mother has demanded that you race a kid she despises. She expects you to whup his ass. You sense the wall before your fingers rake the coarse bumps of the cement. You jump up in the air to right yourself and then slide deep into the water feet first, looking up at the bottom of the pool reflected in the surface tension. In that brief squint of air, you see him already climbing out of the pool. When you surface again, your mother is stooped over her bleacher seat, stuffing her belongings into her bag, getting ready to leave without you.

"You've just gone all the way, for the first time, wearing your manhood like a new pink skin, afraid that it will shine through your clothes

You're 17 years old. You've just gone all the way, for the first time, wearing your manhood like a new pink skin, afraid that it will shine through your clothes. You stand on the porch, studying your reflection in the glass of the screen door. Why didn't you come home later, once your parents were in bed? You try to remember how to breathe. Does it usually sound this loud? Does your chest usually expand this much? You open the door, blinking at how bright the living room lights appear. You edge around the room, but you didn't need to worry; your parents barely realize you're home, much less that you're a man.

You're not so naïve as to believe you'll only get to relive the good things. And anyway, reliving these memories doesn't seem so bad now, does it?

You've been ready to die for a long time.

You just never thought about dying here, on the floor, grit pressing into your palms, your back, your forehead. Little black specks your shoes never told you about but simply ground further into the wood, staining it darker, a greasy grit you now know as if it were trying to crawl into every exposed pore of your body. Little atoms carried on the soles of shoes and boots, from the garden, from the street, from the porch, from other people's lives, now spread across this floor like sand washed ashore a distant beach. Sticking to the wetness of your skin as sweat becomes your ocean. Far away the ceiling harbors its own stains of dirt and tiny bugs caught in stringy webs.

The first time you saw him, you knew your life would change forever. Sometimes late at night you tell yourself it was love at first sight. Sometimes he will even agree. But on that first day, when he made his way across the crowded bull pen and stood at your desk – drawn against his will, he would later tell his friends – waiting for you to look up, feeling some link with destiny, it was not love. Simply a shared premonition.

He's sitting at the kitchen table, which has been pressed up against the window to borrow as much sunlight as possible. In a few hours, when it gets dark, he will half stand, leaning across the table to pull down the shade. He will turn on the delicate fairy of blackened iron holding out its yellowed lampshade as if a gift, little starbursts of mold obscuring the glow in a random pattern, casting small pools of light and shadow onto the green vinyl tablecloth. But right now, the afternoon sun is still enough to illuminate the bills scattered across the table.

You've just come in from mowing the lawn, your T-shirt sticking to your body like a second skin, a covering you never go without, even on the hottest days. You look down, amazed again how every time you mow the grass you somehow become smudged with grease, even when you'd swear that you had never touched the engine. No matter how careful you are, half-formed finger-shaped smudges of brownish green bruise the damp white cotton. Another T-shirt that will not come clean.

The house is hot and close, with an odor only old houses seem to possess. Even with all the doors and windows open. A sheen covers his skin, despite the fact that he's been sitting in here, hidden from the sun, barely moving as he adds up what he owes. What you owe.

Outside the fresh smell of newly cut grass was strong in your nostrils, but in here, that scent is gone until you shrug your shoulder up to wipe your jaw against your arm, grazing damp shirt sleeve and bare skin, breathing in the mixture of grease and grass and sweat, that when you were little reminded you of loosing your stomach when your mother would drive really fast over a small rise in the road. A sensation that you would later recognize as the feeling just before you'd have sex.

Something makes you wish you had waited a little longer on the front porch, shaded from the early afternoon sun bleaching the houses across the street. Where you could feel the coolness radiating up from the cement floor, a chilled border at the edge of the long dark interiors of the house.

Instead, you're here, deep inside, leaning against the kitchen doorway to watch him work. You could go back outside, across the room, through the hallway, out the door in a matter of seconds, unless you're crawling.

Like someone who slips in the back door while you wait at the front, your life flashes before your eyes. But not the way you imagined, not the way you thought. No triumphs or regrets or loves from your past. No years that have come before – only the minutes yet to come.

Because you don't know what you've done this time. And three times seems enough. Even batters are called out after three swings, though his aim is much more precise

Because you don't know what you've done this time. And three times seems enough. Even batters are called out after three swings, though his aim is much more precise. No one knows about the other times, the bruises and abrasions hidden by your hair or along your back.

Four times seem too many. Before he stands, you know the chair will be knocked to the floor by the force of his rising. Before he swings, you know you will not just block his punch, but beat him to it.

Because you've had enough.

Because all the person hitting wants is to be hit.

Your lungs expand to take in all the life they can. Your fists clinch. About to say a single word.

A bomb deadlier than any other.

'No.'

Over his shoulder, the sunlight shines dimly through the roll-up blinds, coating the room in sepia as if it were photograph from when the house was first built. The wallpaper peels in small triangles from each seam as wall meets ceiling.

You realize that the house has tasted of spoiled grapefruit juice for a long time now, long before you came here, bitter. But you kept drinking because you weren't sure you could trust your tongue.

Your eyes scan his face searching for some sign, but the only sign is on the table behind him, the butcher's knife.

From somewhere in the back of your mind, just behind your left ear, you realize he will fight you to the death. Yours or his, it's all the same to him.

The choice is yours. The choices lay before you like the branches of a gnarled tree disappearing into the green depths trying to scrub the sky clean.

He places both hands on your chest and shoves.

In that moment, this is what you see:

You see yourself push back, shoving and punching until he stumbles against the table. You see him pick up the knife, and your mouth makes small "ohs" as he plunges the knife into your chest over and over.

What you do not see is heaven.

Or worse, you see yourself shove him back, pushing and punching until he stumbles against the table, but you know he'll pick up the knife, so you pick it up first, trying to get away, but he keeps lunging at you, trying to turn the knife on you, until finally you stab him without meaning to, his life bleeding out across the kitchen floor.

What you do not see is how many years it will be before you no longer flinch when a lover reaches up to brush the hair from your eyes. You do not see how many years it will be before you can hold a knife without feeling the resistance of flesh, that soft sound more deafening than anything that comes from your mouth.

Your life or his. You want to believe there is another future, another choice. Something you cannot see.

So instead of 'no' you say, 'please.' When he places both hands on your chest and shoves, you do not shove him back, you merely turn. The front door is only nine steps away. You make it to four before he has tackled you to the floor, shoving you down as he kneels on one knee, driving its sharp point into your back as he pushes himself up to full height.

You know better than to stand. So you crawl towards the door. Not a word leaves your mouth, which seems to enrage him more. Droplets fall from your hair, but it no longer matters if they're blood or sweat. It's almost over now.

If you saw a still photograph of this moment, you might think you were sheltered in the safety of sleep, curled up and dreaming. Except this isn't a photograph. His boot is embedding itself in your soft skin, grunts and obscenities yanked from his mouth, as if connected by a string to his swinging foot.

You cover your head, exposing your back more clearly. You feel the arch of your lower spine, how close to the skin it is, how close each kick comes to it. You wonder if your skull would be stronger, but how can you choose between a broken back or a concussion?

You rise up on all fours to crawl a little further, the kicks more frantic, the screen door before you.

Though you don't know it yet, this is the future you have chosen:

Lying in the freshly mown grass, your four-year-old neighbor crouching down beside you as he lays the back of his palm against your forehead and asks if you're not feeling well.

All of your belongings thrown onto the lawn.

Crawling into your car and driving out into a cornfield where you'll lay curled up for hours, staining the cloth seats with blood and sweat and clear fluid that seeps from your wounds.

But right now -

You lift your eyes just enough to see white metal, smooth to the touch, not quite meeting the floor, a crack of sunlight marking the threshold. You know the screen door doesn't latch; the weakest touch will push it open.

You imagine yourself watching from outside, standing in the bright sunlight across the street.

The floor is hot here, worn bare, black with dirt, and all you know for sure is that through that door is the cool touch of concrete and the smell of fresh cut grass. ◨

Double page spread, full colour – £350

Single page, full colour – £200

Half page, full colour – £120

Single page, b&w – £150

Half page, b&w – £70

To take advantage of the above rates and advertise with Hinterland, or to discuss sponsorship or other collaborations, please contact Andrew Kenrick: hinterlandnonfiction@gmail.com

HINTERLAND

HENRIETTA ROSE IN

NEW FI

ANIMALIA PARADOXA
HENRIETTA ROSE-INNES

THIS PARADISE
RUBY COWLING

BOILER
HOUSE
PRESS

4

RUBY COWLING

NES   BEN BOREK

CTION

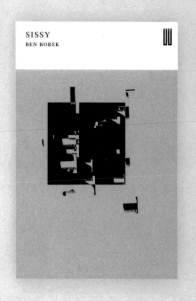

SISSY
BEN BOREK

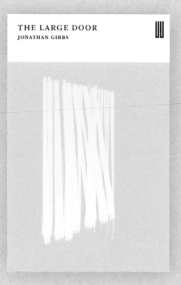

THE LARGE DOOR
JONATHAN GIBBS

4 / 19

JONATHAN GIBBS

IN CONVERSATION WITH
Damian Le Bas

Hinterland editors Andrew Kenrick and Freya Dean sat down with author Damian Le Bas to talk about his recent book, *The Stopping Places: A Journey Through Gypsy Britain*, the perils of writing non-fiction and why we should cherish the value of rhyme in language.

Andrew: What was it about now that made you want to write *The Stopping Places*?

Damian: I'd been working as a journalist, specialising in Gypsy and Traveller issues, and that was really interesting in lots of ways – in terms of the people I met, learning not just about the history of my own background but the wider cultural issues around how Britain and Europe have struggled with minorities and with nomadism. But it was also an incredibly frustrating experience. Part of my job description was to act as the national champion for Gypsies and Travellers in the media, which meant that if there was a controversy it was my task to respond to it. That meant lots of early morning radio interviews, during which the presenters and the producers were quite happy to subject me to racist abuse by the public; straightforward, horribly pernicious stereotypes. I began to feel there was a difference, to how that ethnicity was treated, compared to any other that I could think of. And I think that's because people didn't really believe it was an ethnicity; so there was this paradox running through almost every discourse I tried to participate in and that was down to a dearth of quality information in all media – certainly compared to how it had been in the past. In the nineteenth century there was a great flourishing of work, largely about, not by, Gypsies and Travellers. I immediately think of people like George Borrow, and then in later decades painters like Augustus John and Dame Laura Knight. And then, in the sixties and seventies there was another golden age of broadcasting on Gypsies and Travellers, with influence from the folk movement through people like Peggy Seeger and Ewan Mac Coll, the great maverick radio producer Charles Parker and the documentary filmmaker Philip Donnellan; incredibly subtle, quite brilliant programmes, but by the time I was working as a journalist the stuff that was on telly was *My Big Fat Gypsy Wedding*, which posed as a cutting-edge glimpse at a hidden community, but was full of completely unjustifiable generalisations. So that was part of the background about wanting to write something that was very different to what I was seeing and hearing and reading.

Freya: *The Stopping Places* offers a very universal account of identity and community and the attempt to define one's place within the world. It taps into something that so many of us are grappling with.

DLB: I'm happy you say that because some people have suggested to me with various levels of clarity and innuendo that this book is part of a problematic movement dividing society into ever-smaller groups of inward-looking people, which some people refer to as a culture war. But it manifestly isn't like that. It's a journey away from simplistic nativism towards something else.

FD: There was a scene in the book that really resonated with me, particularly in this new age of walls going up, where you speak cautiously with a man you've just encountered and he almost rebukes you and says 'I don't have any borders.'

DLB: That's because he'd grown up travelling back and forth over the English-Welsh border.

FD: And that captured how I feel. Half my family are Dutch and half are British, and I have the same feeling about the lack of borders.

DLB: There was a tension there between this, the dislike of hard boundaries and binarism that is part of my intellectual makeup and my family background, but also this way that the border is seen as something to be maintained, even a good thing in superstitious terms. There's an uneasy coexistence of times when a division, or a boundary can be helpful, or you might think it is psychologically, and when it becomes bad. We're wrestling with this as a wider culture.

AK: You said you've faced that resistance; have there been other resistances?

DLB: Well I should make it clear that the vast majority of the response has been incredibly warm, but I've had a measure of resistance. Several members of my family believed it was immoral that I was going to write this book – and I hadn't even begun writing at that point, so it didn't matter what the content was – it was the fact I was writing it at all. It's sad when this happens when you're trying to do something that you think is positive and other people don't agree. But at the same time, as a writer and regardless of my background, I have to believe that people have a right to create. So this was a real point of ethical departure for me from certain people in my family. What it led to was for me to spend the first six months after I'd got the deal to write this book, not writing the book I said I was going to write, but writing diary entries attempting to justify the act of writing the book.

AK: It's the question you always encounter as a non-fiction writer: at what point does it stop being your story to tell?

DLB: Even as you're saying that, I'm beginning to think maybe there is an immoral side to it. In some sense I'm still trying to figure that out. I do know these arguments can destroy relationships. And it's very strange to set that against letters I receive from people who feel I've resolved a problem for them. I've had a couple of letters from people who've said 'you're the first person who's articulated the discomfort I feel with my mixed heritage.' To have that bond with somebody you've never met is special, it seems to cast the resistance in an even stranger light. But maybe this is just the way it is with non-fiction. I think it can be with fiction as well, because people read things into it, allusions you've made to characters, but you've got that license that non-fiction writers do not.

AK: But this wasn't your first piece of writing on the subject. How was your book seen as something different?

DLB: Well it was going to refer at length and specifically to my family. What I think we all have in common is the difficulty around that. And hovering in the background there were issues surrounding my right to discuss Romani culture, because even though I grew up in and am descended from it, it's not all of my background. There's also the tension that's been there for a very long time within Romani culture, between those who have made a living through being extrovert and using their ethnicity as part of their livelihood, and that includes fortune tellers, performers and artists, who would use it as an indicator of where they were coming from, in a positive way. And then you've got people who prospered by hiding their heritage, the people who had to lie low. So, a typical Gypsy trade these days might be something like tree surgery, tarmacking or block paving. And I'm sure for many people who do that, they certainly wouldn't shout about being a Gypsy roofing firm, because people have this idea you're going to rip them off. So there's a bit of a divide between people who need or want to hide and those who seek to do the opposite.

FD: The book is so beautifully written, there are whole passages that are such a joy to read – but how did you arrive at that? Perhaps it's not helpful to draw distinctions between creative non-fiction and journalism, because they're all forms of writing, but how did you start writing in this style?

DLB: For me there is a clear distinction, because my day job was working as a journalist and I was very much in the habit of writing factual news pieces with the how, what, where, why in a certain order. And then my – I can't really say my night job, that sounds slightly louche – my real passion was poetry, and I was getting some work as a gigging poet and had published a couple of poems.

FD: That's interesting, as the writing has a real ear for those tiny details that are so particular to poetry, and the way you tease them out to assume real meaning.

DLB: In terms of the style, I think it's influenced both by being someone who writes a lot of poetry, as well as a love for deliberately rhythmic writing. I love rhyme, and it upsets me that rhyme is actively stigmatised at the moment. There's good rhyme and cheesy rhyme, but to take a device and say it's bad is never justifiable. I always think of a poem by Don Paterson called Sliding on Loch Ogil, which he wrote in response to the suggestion that you shouldn't use words ending in 'ing' in poetry. It's a brilliant short poem, starting—

Remember, brother soul, that day spent cleaving
Nothing from nothing like a thrown knife?

That's a perfect illustration for me of why you should take on these absurd proclamations and smash them. And most of my first loves in literature are very rhythmic and iambic or, in the case of Gerard Manley Hopkins, experimentations with that form, the sprung rhythm in his case, or the way Emily Dickinson composes or suggests rhythm in her poetry. So that has always mattered to me and I think *The Stopping Places* is quite iambic, particularly for a non-fiction book.

In terms of the imagery and that attention to detail that you noticed, perhaps that reflects on the kind of stuff I was reading at the time, which wasn't really literature about Gypsies – I'd read an awful lot about and by Gypsy, Roma and Traveller people, so by the time I set out on the road, it was a wider range of material about the landscape that was beginning to obsess me. The books that were dearest to me when I was writing this were *The Outrun* by Amy Liptrot, *The Living Mountain* by Nan Shepherd, *Travels with Charlie* by John Steinbeck and *Consolations of the Forest* by Sylvain Tesson. They were the books I kept returning to. And none of them are about Romani culture at all. They don't necessarily have that much in common, though they're all non-fiction books with elements including but not limited to travel, redemption, freedom, rebirth. The sometimes impossible attempt to distil large things into short descriptions.

AK: Your book reminded me a lot of the new British nature writing. There's an overlap with Roger Deakin, for example.

DLB: I was reading *Wildwood*, too, and Robert Macfarlane. It's steeped in that. I come from a particular place and that's what this book is about, people being connected to the cycles of the places they're from. There's not a chance I'd have written *The Stopping Places* if it wasn't for the resurgence of people writing about the British landscape. It is as indebted to that as anything that's overtly about Gypsy stuff, in my opinion.

To return to our discussion of the difficulties of writing non-fiction, some of the understandable but misguided questions people ask play on my mind. They say to you 'did everything in this book really happen?' And I think, are you asking me if this is a fundamentally honest work, to which I can answer yes. Or are you asking me if it would stand up in a police interrogation, in which case I'm not entirely sure how to answer that, because I might have mistakenly recollected the sequence of events, for instance. I mention dreams I had: did they happen? Well they certainly happened in my mind. There are references to monsters in there that I was told about as a kid. Do they exist? Well they existed for me at the time. So I'm really wary of the idea that non-fiction has to be held accountable to a forensic standard that other kinds of writing are not. I think that it has to be true; it can't be a pack of lies. But these aren't accounts of scientific experiments written in a dispassionate language, which is attempting to get away from the expansive. And as Steinbeck says in *Travels with Charlie*, or words to this effect, someone on the same journey as him at the exact same time in the same vehicle would have written a completely different account of the trip, never mind someone who makes the journey ten years later.

But are people really up for having this conversation? I think it's disturbing to a lot of people to think there's more to it than a simply given account, a hand-on-the-holy-book testimony. I think that's what lots of people think they want from the genre.

FD: It's not that simple, or else every book would come with a meticulously footnoted biography.

DLB: I describe encounters with people I met. I described them as I remember them. But, say, someone comes across as slightly sinister because of the way I've confected the prose or even how I've presented the dialogue. But I might be misunderstanding that person. They might have grown up with a different set of gestures and body language to me. I worry about this stuff. Have I made someone look like they were being nasty when they weren't, when I was getting the wrong end of the stick. It's a microcosm around the issues about being human.

FD: That sensibility comes through in the book.

AK: Were you ever tempted to write this as a work of fiction. Did you feel it might be easier if you wrote it as a novel?

DLB: By the end of the book I did start thinking about how exhilarating it might be to make things up, and the idea of fiction suddenly seemed transgressive and dangerous and edgy to me in a way that it hadn't before. Previously I'd just felt cowed by what I think is the greater cultural reverence for fiction writers over non-fiction writers, and which makes me, perhaps unjustifiably, more wary about embarking on adventures in fiction. I feel like I've got my head around what is required of a travel book, but I've not got my head around what a novel could be. My favourite novels are long and expansive and complex works, which came late in a writer's life. Perhaps it's just as hard to write a travel book and I was just naive about that, and naivety facilitates action. But I feel like when someone says "we have with us a novelist" that still carries a prestige that is slightly different to 'we have in our midst a writer.' Will Self has said that the prestige of the novelist is waning, but I think it's still there.

AK: Let me rephrase my question – were you ever tempted to write it just as Romani history, and leave out the memoir?

DLB: The publishers have classified this as memoir/travel. For some reason I shiver at the word memoir, especially when it's someone like me who hasn't really done anything, but it contains personal and family reminiscence so that's fair enough, at the technical level. Travel I was perfectly happy with.

AK: But it could have easily been labelled history or culture, or society. It could have gone on any number of bookshelves in the shop.

DLB: I'd agree. This was advice from my first editor on the book, Parisa Ebrahimi. She said I was trying to keep three plates spinning at the same time. One of them was memoiristic, it was about family history; the other was about Romani history, so a much wider purview; and the third was about this journey that I took. She rather charmingly talked about the need to keep them all spinning, and that when someone does that they have to know when to move from one stick to the other. And the real headache for me was trying to manage those transitions. Sometimes it seemed to happen by itself, and sometimes I felt I was employing very forced devices to make it happen, which hopefully are largely invisible.

AK: What was your process? Had you decided to go on the journey before you wrote the book, or did you decide to write the book before you went on the journey?

DLB: My book grew out of an essay, called 'Stopping Places,' that I was cajoled, reluctantly, into writing by a friend of mine for the *Junket*, an online magazine. Parts of that essay remain in the book. Since I was a kid I've been obsessed with these places where my family used to live. I was jealous that they'd had this life that I'd not partaken in; but also felt that in a way it was mine, at one remove, because they'd painted such a picture of it that lived in my mind. And I started making trips to these places, without any real logical justification. I just felt drawn to them. The essay came from that. I had no idea then that it might grow into a book.

FD: Did you keep notes, when you were on the journey. Or a diary?

DLB: I've kept a diary on and off since I was a teenager and that was sort of ramped up by the process of doing this. Sometimes I'd record my thoughts on a dictaphone as I pulled up somewhere. If I was driving and had an urgent thought, and my wife Candice happened to be with me, I'd ask her to record what I was saying, because I was scared of losing it. Because you might remember in vague terms the thought you had, but the fear is always that you lose that precise formulation of words that had first crystallised it.

AK: To what extent did you plan your route in response to the shape you wanted the book to have?

DLB: I'd already done some of these journeys before I'd got the book deal. And indeed some of the ones referred to are places I visited as a child, the horse fairs for example. There's a fair bit of ground I'd have covered anyway but then there are some places I wouldn't have gone to without knowing I wanted to write about them. There's no way I'd have spent the amount of time in laybys and out of the way places where Travellers have lived in the past if it weren't for writing this book. I'd have continued to be magnetised to the places where the culture lives now rather than where it used to exist. That massively affected the kind of travelling I was doing, and was what led to me living in my van for most of a year.

AK: Have you carried on doing some of these journeys since you finished writing?

DLB: I fetishise travelling and living in vehicles a lot less than I used to. This is something that I quite proudly share with other people who've done a good bit of that. You have a slightly more wry look in your eye when someone extolls the virtues of living on the move. And that's living it the easy way with modern vehicles, not in bender tents – and without children. I was also earning a living in a job that I could do inside, under shelter. When you write you can stay out of the rain. If you're a roofer or you're out picking vegetables, you don't have that luxury. So many things conspired to make this easier for me than for most Travellers, and to make it in some ways a facile or even a false simulacrum of that way of life. That's why I tried to make it clear that I was trying to do something different to that, and I used the Romani word dinlo to describe it, which is a necessary self-deprecation.

AK: That's one of the things that came through in the book; as well as the passion for the landscape, the passion for the language. Was the language something you've always had an interest in?

DLB: I love language, and always have. I love the Romani language, and always have.

FD: You weave that language in so well, because you don't over explain it. Some writers use language that isn't easy to understand without recourse to a relevant dictionary, but you weave it in so naturally that the meaning is always clear. Did you have to work hard at that aspect?

DLB: I was wary of putting in excerpts written in florid Romani, which would then require a footnote and take the reader out of the narrative. One friend of mine – a writer, William Kraemer – always says how much it annoys him when the writer presumes the reader can speak French, say, in an English book and a translation isn't given. And it not only takes you out of what you're reading, in some cases it can turn you against the writer. So I wanted, where possible, to retain the flow.

I didn't want to include a glossary at first. I thought if I can get away with it it'd be fantastic for several reasons. And I'll admit that one of them is that having a glossary of Romani words opened me up to this banal but still hurtful accusation that I was giving away our language. And some Travellers do think that; that it's a cultural betrayal to translate our language. But it's a mis-founded idea. Firstly there have been excellent, thorough dictionaries of the Romani language available for centuries, so if you want to learn it you can. Secondly I think it's highly unlikely that someone's going to suddenly obtain a kind of fluency in it just by reading a book – would that that were the case! And thirdly, I don't think it's bad. I don't think it's bad if people that aren't from a culture acquire a bit of the language of a different culture. In fact it opens dialogue, friendship, even love, marriage; good things grow out of that. And I know a lot of Gypsy people feel very passionate about their language and the need to preserve it, and sometimes it's useful to be able to exclude people from what you're saying, but I think if we generally apply that perspective to language we've all had it.

AK: It seems like you often use it in the book when you're encountering another Romani speaker, you use it as a bridge rather than a divide.

DLB: Exactly. And also there's massive ambiguity here about where those divides are and what they are. Because often I was using a form of Romani that isn't my native language to connect with Roma people who are from a very different cultural background to me. So am I then using a foreign language? Well, I'm using a sister dialect to my own, but I didn't grow up speaking Lovari Romani, or Kalderash Romani, but I've attempted to acquire a bit of those languages to connect with other Romani people. But I don't see that as intrinsically different to a child learning French or Mandarin at school. But somehow the rules aren't always evenly applied when it comes to minority languages. So something I talk about in the book is this implication that in Britain you must learn these traditionally rural, minority languages authentically; at the knee of an often idyllically portrayed, illiterate rural person. You can learn English from books, that's fine, but you must learn Cornish or Romani or Manx authentically. What does authentically mean? Are books not authentic? These questions really interest me. There are many double standards, often unconsciously applied when we talk about this stuff.

AK: Did you ever worry, having written this book, about being pegged as a spokesperson for Romani culture?

DLB: Well that's something that happens. It doesn't sit easily for me, because I don't think I'm a spokesperson in the first instance, and in the second our culture doesn't really like the idea of spokespersons. We're suspicious of people who get on a pedestal to speak. But what I was worried about was being pigeonholed as someone who only wrote about Gypsies, and that's a risk you take when you bring autobiographical material into your work. It's a risk I was obviously willing to take.

FD: So do you have a next project in mind?

DLB: I've got a couple, which I hope you'll forgive me for being superstitious about discussing. Some of it is Romani related and some of it isn't. At least not overtly. I'm interested in all manner of things, the land, the sea, the air, literature, life in general. But that's something that worries me – is this writer a one-trick pony? I hope that's not the case, otherwise my career's going to be rubbish.

The paperback edition of *The Stopping Places* is out now from Vintage. **H**

Like what you've read?

Look out for the second issue of Hinterland, on sale August 2019. Better still, sign up for a subscription and get our next batch of stand-out writing delivered direct to your door, desktop or tablet.

Annual print & digital subscription £34
Four issues, saving £6 off list price

Annual digital subscription £16
Four issues, saving £4 off list price

Subscribers also enjoy the benefits of being able to submit their writing to Hinterland free of charge.

Visit our website to subscribe:

www.hinterlandnonfiction.com/subscribe